4.25

Basics of Business

The M & E Handbook Series

Basics of Business

David Lewis BSc (Econ)

Pitman Publishing
128 Long Acre, London WC2E 9AN

A Longman Group Company

British Library Cataloguing in Publication Data

Lewis, David, *1938–*
Basics of business.
1. Business studies
I. Title
658

ISBN 0 7121 0794 0

Founding Editor: P W D Redmond

Typeset, printed and bound in Great Britain

Contents

Part four People and business

Part five Aid and control

Preface

This *Handbook* provides the basis for a comprehensive understanding of today's business environment. Information relating to business institutions and activities is presented in a simple and uncomplicated way, in the hope that it will be a ready source of reference for both the general reader and students on many different business courses.

Topics are defined and built up in logical order, and cross-referenced to allow quick and easy access to items, while progress tests at the end of chapters should enable students to test their understanding and help with examination revision. In order to encourage the reader to think about the issues raised in the text, actual examples have been included at the end of chapters in the form of case studies.

The book provides a framework for GCSE in Business Studies, within which students of a wide range of ability will be able to develop their understanding and knowledge of business. Additionally, the book will prove useful for courses such as BTEC, LCC, RSA, and PEI.

I would like to thank the following organizations for supplying information upon which material in the book has been based: Austin Rover, British Aerospace, Cadbury-Schweppes, the Hotel and Catering Training Board, Marks and Spencer Plc, Massey-Ferguson, National Westminster Bank Plc, Telecom Gold Limited, Tesco, and Josiah Wedgwood & Sons Limited.

Finally, my thanks to Ann, Jane, and Nia for their help, encouragement, and invaluable support.

DBL
1988

Part one

The business environment

1

Economic framework

Nature of the economic problem

1. Introduction. Economics is the study of how people seek to obtain as much satisfaction as possible from limited resources. Individuals demand more and better goods and services, firms compete for a greater share of a market, and governments strive to ensure that a country enjoys a higher standard of living than other countries. Equally, however, we have to accept that the resources available to us are limited, whether they be minerals in the ground or money in our pay packets. We are all constantly dealing with the problem of choosing between conflicting demands upon our money and resources.

2. Some basic definitions.

(*a*) *Wants*. Our wants may be in the form of goods we need or services we wish to obtain. Our wants include a range of requirements – basic necessities such as food and shelter; things we may take for granted such as a car and television; or luxuries such as a rather extravagant holiday . In economic terms we talk of the 'satisfaction' we derive from obtaining these wants.

(*b*) *Scarcity*. This is the central problem of economics – by which we have to accept that the goods we want are always in limited supply and cannot meet our demands upon them. This is true in almost every sense – the earth's resources of energy and raw materials are finite and our own incomes are never enough to satisfy the demands we place upon them.

(*c*) *Choice*. This is the compromise we have to accept between unlimited wants and limited resources. Choice is forced upon everyone – individuals can afford either to buy a new car or take a holiday; a county council can build either a new school or a hospital; or the government of a country has to choose between a new defence system or better welfare services.

(*d*) *Opportunity cost*. This is the real cost, in economic terms, of what we choose to consume, i.e. our loss at what we have to forego. Thus we accept that the real cost to us of our new car is the holiday we have to go without this year, or that the cost of our country's improved defences will be our dissatisfaction with welfare provision.

Interdependence

3. Definition. In a modern economy, everyone is both a producer and a consumer, and both roles are basic to the interdependence of our way of life. Whereas in times past we all would have been more-or-less self-sufficient, providing for our own needs, today we insist upon having a wide range of goods from which to choose. In the same way, everyone is willing to work at highly specialized jobs in order to produce a variety of goods and services. As economies develop, people, organizations, and countries become increasingly more interdependent – individuals work at a specific job and share in the benefits of the production of fellow workers; firms manufacture a specific product and rely upon other firms to supply them with raw materials and to distribute that product; and countries engage in trading goods with other countries to the advantage of everyone.

4. Specialization. Interdependence has developed as we have progressed from self-sufficiency to specialization. Specialization may be:

(*a*) *by product*, as in the early days of the Industrial Revolution when workers in a factory would be solely concerned in the production of a single commodity; or

(*b*) *by process*, as workers in a factory became individually responsible for a specific operation within the overall production.

5. Division of Labour. The specialization of labour into distinctive processes is called the division of labour. It is the basis of a modern industrial society in which most forms of labour have become highly specialized, and has resulted in a considerable increase in the total output of goods and services.

(*a*) The advantages of the division of labour are:

(*i*) a worker can be employed in the job for which he has the greatest aptitude and thus make a greater contribution to production;

(*ii*) concentration upon a single operation develops skill;

(*iii*) it cuts down on time lost, for example, in training or changing operations;

(*iv*) specialized equipment can be more easily introduced and used more intensively.

(*b*) The division of labour does, however, bring with it certain disadvantages:

(*i*) the monotonous routine of many production line jobs develops boredom in workers;

(*ii*) fewer workers may be needed as output increases;

(*iii*) a highly specialized worker is more vulnerable to unemployment if conditions change, for example by the introduction of a new machine;

(*iv*) increased interdependence means that any disruption, for example a strike by one body of workers, may have widespread results.

Economic systems

6. Introduction. With the development of the interdependent community, decisions have always to be made by both the producers and consumers within it. The basic economic problem of unlimited wants has to be balanced by the limited resources available to meet those demands. Producers, on the one hand, have to decide what goods to produce, at what price, and in what market, while consumers have the problem of choosing between a variety of products upon which to spend their money. The ways in which decisions are made by the community in allocating resources determines the type of economic system that results.

7. Types of system. There are three main types of economic system:

(*a*) *The market economy*, in which decisions are made freely by individuals, using the price system to decide upon the nature and quantity of goods produced and which consumers obtain them. This is the basis upon which most western countries have developed their economies.

(*b*) *The command* (or *planned*) *economy* in which decisions are made by the central government or agencies appointed by them. Most command economies are found in communist states.

(*c*) *The mixed economy* in which elements of both the market economy and the command economy are found. Many of the western nations, for example the UK, have now developed a mixed economy in which some decisions upon allocation are made by the price system, while other decisions have become the responsibility of the government or other authorities. In Britain, individuals are free to choose the job at which they work and the goods they buy, but the government intervenes in many ways such as by providing services, running nationalized industries, or by controlling or regulating aspects of business. In the mixed economy there is therefore a private sector in which decisions are largely made by the price mechanism, while there is also a public sector in which decisions are made by the state.

The market economy

8. Introduction. In the market economy, resources are allocated by the price mechanism, by which a balance is maintained between the demands of consumers and the willingness of producers to supply. In order to understand how the price mechanism works we need to examine the nature of markets, and the forces of demand and supply.

9. The market. The market, in economic terms, is where buyers and sellers meet in order to exchange goods. It may not exist in physical terms, but may simply refer to the demand for a particular commodity, for example we talk of the market for compact-disc players or for kitchen equipment. It may vary considerably in size, for example, the market for oil is international while a village newsagent's market would be the immediate locality. Improvements in communications and technological developments have made many markets international, for example, trading in stocks and shares on international stock exchanges is now almost entirely conducted by computerized links between dealers.

10. Demand. Demand for a commodity is defined as being the wish to buy that commodity backed up by a willingness to pay for it. It is often referred to as 'effective demand' to emphasise the point that desire to possess a commodity has to be accompanied by the willingness and ability to pay a certain price for it. Whilst we as consumers will have a demand for a particular commodity, in business terms we are more interested in the 'market demand' for that commodity – that is, the total amount of it that will be bought. Demand has to be expressed in terms of time and price, for example, the demand for a particular type of motor car might be for 100 per month at a price of £8,000.

A table of the market demand for a certain product at different prices can be constructed from individual demand curves, and the information presented in the form of a demand curve. The typical result of the demand schedules for many products is that the demand curve will slope downwards from left to right, indicating that consumers are willing to buy more of a product as its price drops, and less as its prices rises. Figure 1.1 shows the demand schedule and curve for 'Chocobite' chocolate bars. At a price of 30 pence, for example, consumers would demand 5,000 bars per week.

11. Changes in demand. The demand for a commodity is determined by several factors:

(*a*) its price;

(*b*) the price of other commodities, for example, if the price of cars rose it is probable that the demand for petrol would fall as fewer cars would be bought and thus less petrol would be required. A rise in the price of a commodity such as butter, on the other

Market demand schedule for 'Chocobite'	
Price (pence)	Quantity demanded per week
50	1,000
40	3,000
30	5,000
20	7,000
10	9,000

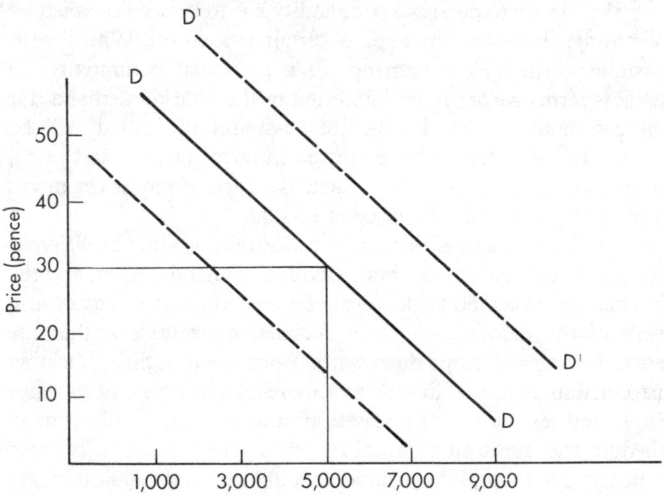

Figure 1.1 *Demand schedule and curve for 'Chocobite' chocolate bars*

hand, might result in an increase in the demand for margarine which would be a substitute for it;

(*c*) the income of consumers will affect demand as a rise in real income will usually result in an increase in demand;

(*d*) taste and fashion may change, typically in clothing for example, and will affect the demand for many products.

We have seen that a change in its own price will cause movements along the demand curve, as in Fig. 1.1. A change in any of the conditions above, however, will result in a movement of the demand curve. If consumers income rose, for example, or if eating chocolate became more popular, then more 'Chocobite' would be demanded at every price, resulting in the movement of the demand curve to D1 in Fig. 1.1.

12. Supply. The supply of a commodity is the amount of a certain good that sellers are willing to produce at a given price. A supply scedule can be drawn up in the same way as the demand schedule referred to above. The combined production of all firms supplying the market with a certain good over a period of time at a certain price can be drawn as a graph (*see* Fig. 1.2). It can be seen that it will typically slope downwards from right to left, indicating for example, that at a higher price producers will be willing to supply more 'Chocobite', while if the market price drops they will wish to reduce the amount they produce.

13. Changes in supply. The supply of a commodity is determined by several factors:

(*a*) The price which the supplier is able to get for the product.

(*b*) The costs of production. If production costs rise, producers will normally wish to supply a smaller quantity, while if costs of production fall then producers are usually prepared to supply increased quantities. Changes in technology will often result in lowering of production costs.

(*c*) The price of other products. If the price of another product increases, producers may decide to switch to producing that product. For example, a farmer may stop growing wheat because a rise in the price of another crop such as barley may make it more profitable for land to be transferred to growing barley.

(*d*) A number of other factors may affect the supply of a commodity, such as the level of taxation, subsidies from the government, or business confidence.

We have seen that as the price of a product changes, the amount supplied of that product at any price is reflected in the supply

Market supply schedule for 'Chocobite'	
Price (pence)	Quantity supplied per week
50	9,000
40	7,000
30	5,000
20	3,000
10	1,000

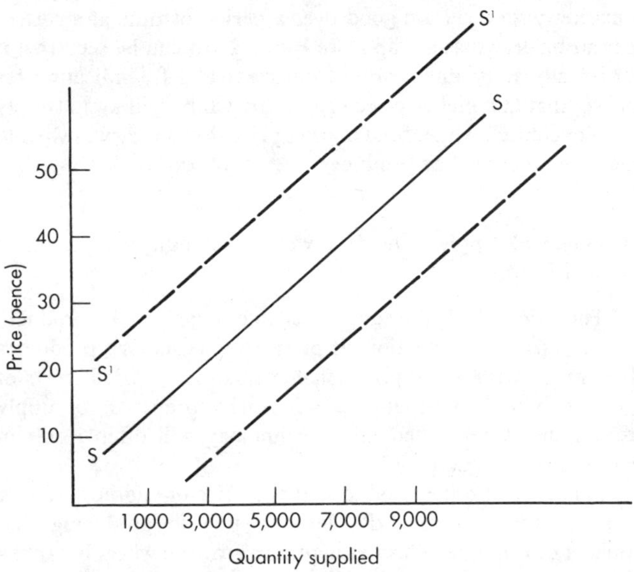

Figure 1.2 *Supply schedule for 'Chocobite'*

curve. If any of the conditions of supply above change, however, then a movement of the supply curve will result. If the price of other chocolate products rises, for example, or a tax is imposed on chocolate bars, then manufacturers of 'Chocobite' might decide to reduce their production to S^1 in Fig. 1.2.

14. Price. Figure 1.3 shows demand and supply curves for 'Chocobite' plotted on the same graph. The demand curve shows how much of the product consumers will buy at each price and the supply curve shows how much of the product suppliers are willing to supply at each price. The point at which they cross is called the *equilibrium* as it is the point at which the forces of demand and supply are equal. This is therefore the market price for that product.

If, instead of the market being in equilibrium, the price was 40 pence, then there would be an excess supply as suppliers would be happy to produce more (7,000 bars per week). Consumers, however, would be willing to take only 3,000 bars at that price. The excess supply will usually result in prices beginning to fall and supply being reduced, so that demand and supply will move back towards the equilibrium position. Similarly, if the price was 20 pence then there would be an excess demand for 'Chocobite' as at that price consumers would like to buy 7,000 bars per week but manaufacturers would only supply 3,000 bars. Because of so many consumers wishing to buy the product, the price can be raised, and will tend to move back to the equilibrium position.

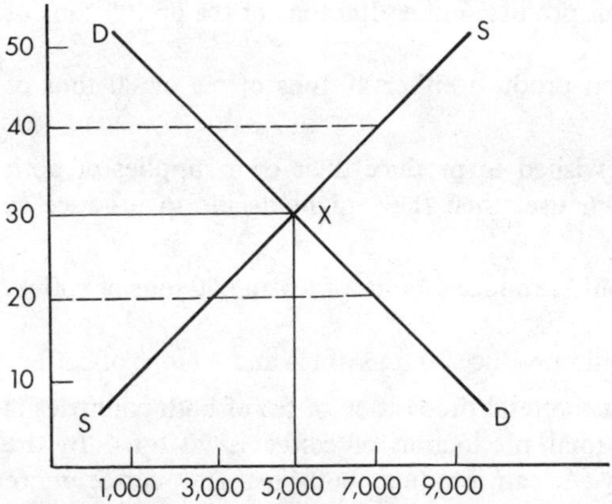

Figure 1.3 *Market price of 'Chocobite'*

International interdependence

15. Introduction. As a country develops specialization, firstly by product and then by process, so too does *interdependence* become international, as countries produce and exchange a wide variety of products. By participating in international trade a country is able to obtain goods which it is unable to produce for itself. Britain, for example, does not have reserves of ores such as tin, and is unable to produce many kinds of fruit such as oranges because of its climate.

16. Comparative advantage. The main reason for international trade taking place lies in the advantages to be found in the theory of *comparative advantage*. This states that it is in the interests of all countries for each country to specialize in the production of those goods and services which it is able to produce more cheaply and efficiently than other countries. By doing so, the benefits of specialization and division of labour are extended worldwide, and the result should be an increase in world production which can then be shared among all countries.

The theory can be explained by assuming that there exist only two countries, both able to produce just two commodities – tea and coffee. Within a certain period of time and with the resources of land, labour, and capital available:

> Country A can produce either 100 tons of tea or 100 tons of coffee, and
> Country B can produce either 40 tons of tea or 80 tons of coffee.

If both countries wished to produce their own supplies of both crops for their own use, then they might decide to produce as follows:

> Country A could produce 50 tons of tea and 50 tons of coffee, and
> Country B could produce 20 tons of tea and 40 tons of coffee.

It can be seen that the total production of tea of both countries is 70 tons and the total production of coffee is 90 tons. In the example, Country A can produce both tea and coffee more efficiently than Country B, and is therefore said to have an *absolute advantage* over Country B. But you will note that it is more efficient at producing tea (producing 50 tons to Country B's 20 tons) than it is at producing coffee (Country B only produces 10 tons less). Thus Country A is said to have a *comparative advantage* in the production of tea, and so in order to obtain the benefits of comparative advantage, Country A should concentrate upon producing tea and allow Country B to specialize in the production of coffee. The position will then be:

Country A will produce 100 tons of tea, and
Country B will produce 80 tons of coffee.

It can be seen that by specialization, the total production of tea has now risen to 100 tons (instead of the previous 70 tons) while the total production of coffee has dropped slightly from 90 tons to 80 tons. Thus, even though Country B is less efficient at producing both crops, overall total production can be increased by specialization and then exchange of products.

17. Terms of trade. In order to obtain the benefits of specialization, Country A and Country B will have to enter into a trading relationship with each other. The rate at which one country will exchange its goods with another country is called the *terms of trade*. It can be measured by calculating the ratio of export prices to import prices.

18. Free trade. Free trade, in which goods move freely between nations, is usually regarded as being of benefit to all countries and many attempts are made to achieve it. The advantages of free trade are:

(*a*) resources throughout the world are used to maximum advantage because of the *theory of comparative costs*;

(*b*) because the market is a world market the advantages of large-scale production can be gained;

(*c*) consumers enjoy wider choice, and standards of living may rise.

19. Restrictions on trade. Despite the advantages of free trade, however, countries will usually place restrictions upon foreign imports in order to protect their own producers from competition. This is termed *protectionism* and may take several forms:

(*a*) *tariffs*, which are taxes imposed upon imported goods;

(*b*) *import quotas*, which are limits upon the quantity of foreign products which can be imported;

(*c*) *exchange controls* on the foreign currency necessary to pay for imports;

(*d*) *controls* upon the specification of foreign goods, such as safety or health requirements;

(*e*) *subsidies* provided by governments to home producers to reduce their costs in competition with foreign goods.

20. Arguments for protectionism. The main reasons for a country to impose restrictions upon trade with other nations are:

(*a*) to protect home industries, especially developing industries;

(*b*) to ensure that a country is reasonably self-sufficient by being able to provide sufficient foodstuffs or to be able to defend itself;

(*c*) to protect a country's standard of living, for example from cheap foreign goods;

(*d*) to restore an adverse balance of payments by reducing imports.

21. World trade. For much of this century countries have imposed barriers upon trade with other countries. Several steps have been taken in an attempt to create free trade between nations by removal of many of these barriers.

(*a*) The General Agreement on Tariffs and Trade (GATT) was signed in 1947 and now has over 70 member nations committed to reducing tariffs and other barriers to trade. It has operated mainly by 'rounds' of general tariff reductions, such as the Kennedy Round, Tokyo Round, and the 1988 Uraguay Round.

(*b*) A number of trading blocs have been formed for free trade between certain countries. The European Community (EC) was formed initially as a customs union to develop free trade between the original six member nations, and is now the largest trading group in the world with twelve member countries. COMECON was formed by East European nations to develop social and economic integration, and CARICOM was set up for economic co-operation in the Caribbean.

22. The Third World. *The Third World* is the term used to define those countries which are economically underdeveloped. It includes many countries in Africa and Asia which have a range of problems such as low incomes, high population, and food shortages. The advanced industrialized nations generally provide foreign aid to help these countries to develop, and to encourage trading links with them. The World Bank is the largest source of finance for developing countries (*see* 2:28).

23. International money. Trade between countries requires that provision has to be made for payments to be made in a variety of different currencies. It is necessary therefore that currencies have their value expressed in terms of other currencies, and the price of one currency in terms of another is called the *exchange rate*. Exchange rates result from the forces of demand and supply for currencies, and foreign exchange dealers in the world's financial centres with telephone and computer links buy and sell currencies daily. If there is strong demand for a currency then its price will rise compared to other currencies, so that exchange rates are constantly fluctuating on the world's exchanges. The US dollar is often used as a yardstick against which other currencies are measured, but today it is usual for the pound sterling to be measured against other currencies such as the German mark and French franc as well.

The EMS (European Monetary System) was set up in 1979 to promote monetary stability in Europe. It is an exchange rate mechanism, with a monetary unit – the ECU – based upon a 'basket' of national currencies, including the pound.

Britain and international trade

24. Background. Despite being a small and heavily populated country (with about one per cent of the world's population) Britain is the fifth largest trading nation in the world. Furthermore, it is a member of the European Community, the world's largest trading area.

Britain has been a major trading nation for many centuries, especially since the early years of the Industrial Revolution when it became the 'Workshop of the World' exporting manufactured goods from its developing factories. A balance has normally been maintained between the export of manufactured goods such as vehicles, machinery, chemicals, electrical and electronic equipment, and the import of foodstuffs and raw materials for industry. Britain is an important oil exporter from the North Sea fields, while a major strength in international trade is the expertise in services such as insurance and banking. Figure 1.4 shows the UK's main exports and the main countries to which they are exported. Figure 1.5 shows the UK's main imports and where they came from.

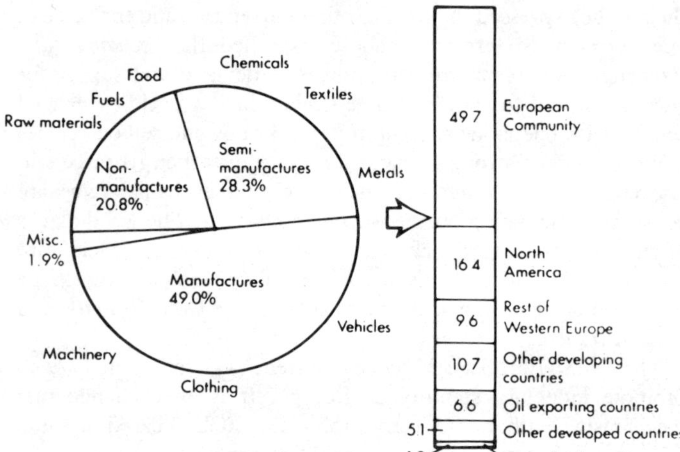

Figure 1.4 *Britain's exports and their destinations (as per cent, 1987)*

25. The balance of payments. The balance of payments is the relationship between payments received for exports to other countries and the payments made to other countries for imports. There is inevitably a gap between any country's receipts and its payments, and this is the balance of payments. It is calculated firstly by measuring the country's balance of trade, that is, the income and expenditure on *visible* goods such as cars, oil, and machinery. *Invisible* items – services such as banking and insurance, and

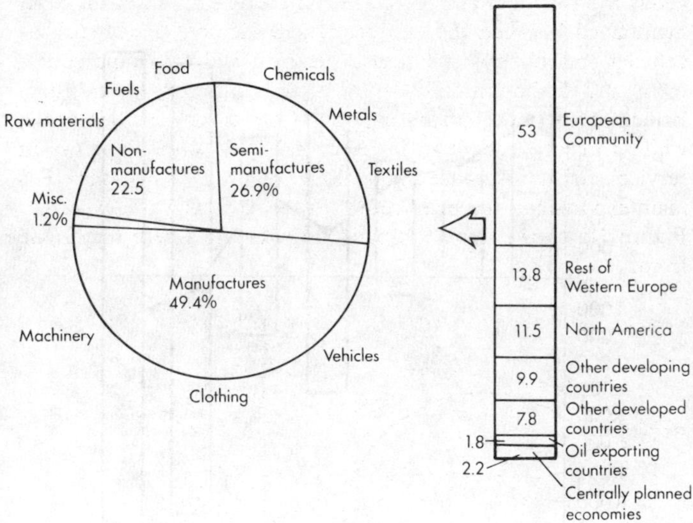

Figure 1.5 *Britain's imports and their sources (as per cent, 1987)*

investments in foreign countries – are then added to arrive at the balance of payments. If payments to other countries are higher than receipts there is a deficit balance while there may be a favourable balance of payments if there is a surplus of a country's exports over imports.

Britain's exports of manufactured goods have fallen in recent years, and in 1983 it recorded, for the first time, a deficit in trade with the rest of the world in manufactures. Figure 1.6 shows trends in Britain's balance of payments in recent years.

Case 1 Airbus Industrie

Airbus Industrie is the consortium established by four major aircraft manufacturers in the UK, France, Federal Republic of Germany, and Spain. The joint venture was intended to challenge the USA supremacy of firms such as Boeing by pooling the resources of the European firms involved – British Aerospace,

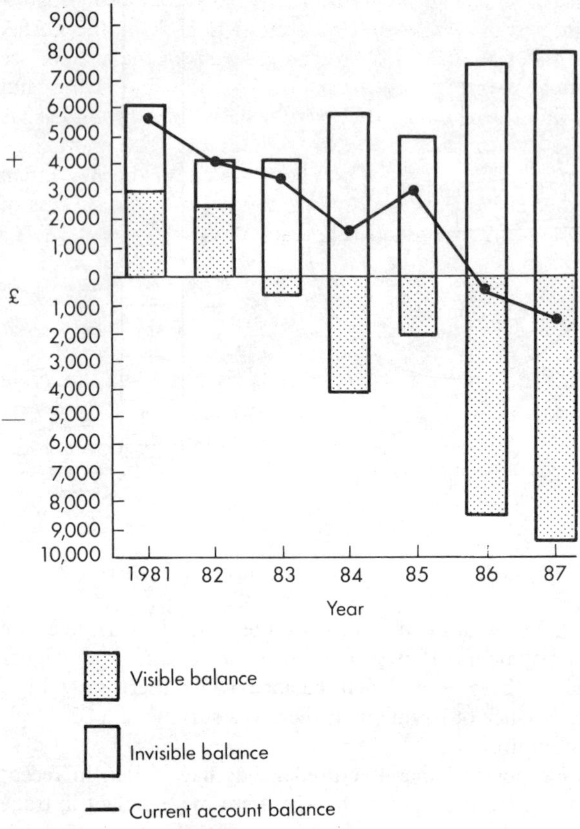

Figure 1.6 *Britain's balance of payments 1981–7*

Aerospatiale of France, Deutsche Airbus of Germany, and CASA of Spain. The latest aircraft to be produced by the consortium is the A320 Airbus, a 150 seat, medium range airliner with many advanced technological features.

Production of the aircraft is shared between the four firms in the consortium. The wings are made in the UK, and a number of factories contribute at various stages to their manufacture before they are built at Chester and finally assembled at Filton in Bristol.

The fuselage is made at Hamburg in Germany, and also at Saint-Nazaire in France, while the tail section is built at the CASA factory at Madrid in Spain. The separate parts of the airliner are brought to Toulouse in France for final assembly and fitting, and there it is flight tested and equipped for delivery to customers. A year before it enters service with airlines in 1988, more pre-production orders and options had been placed for the A320 than for any other aircraft ever built – an indication of the success of this example of international co-operation.

Progress test 1

1. What do we hope to understand by studying economics? (**1**)
2. Define: wants, scarcity, choice, and opportunity cost. (**2**)
3. What do you understand by the term *interdependence*? (**3**)
4. What is *specialization*? (**4**)
5. What are the advantages and disadvantages of division of labour? (**5**)
6. Describe the main types of economic system. (**7**)
7. What do you understand by *the market*? (**8**)
8. Describe how price is determined in a free market economy. (**14**)
9. What advantages can be gained from international trade? (**16**)
10. What restrictions may prevent free trade taking place? (**19**)
11. What developments have been made towards free trade? (**21**)
12. In what products, and with which countries, does the UK trade? (**24**)
13. What is the balance of payments? (**25**)
14. What have been the main trends in the UK's balance of payments? (**25**)
15. What was the main reason for establishing Airbus Industrie? (**Case 1**)
16. How interdependent are the four firms building the Airbus? (**Case 1**)

2

The role of government

Introduction

1. Definition. Government is concerned with the way in which we organize ourselves. If a country is be run effectively, its government must have powers to make laws in the interests of all and to ensure that they are carried out fairly. In the western world we are proud of our democracies within which people are free and equal and can go about their lives without undue interference from government but within the protection of the state.

2. Development. The rights which we enjoy today, however, were earned with difficulty. For many years it was assumed that the ruler of a state held complete authority, but the French Revolution's call for 'Liberty, Equality, and Fraternity' demanded that the rights of individuals be respected. The famous call for a government 'by the people, of the people, and for the people' at the time of the establishment of the USA is an indication of what we expect from our system of government in the modern world.

3. Importance to business. It is the role of government to ensure the existence of an environment within which business can flourish. In Britain, the stability of our system of government developed over many centuries has provided a framework for business development. Initially, the maintenance of law and order was accepted as being the sole responsibility of government, but today governments have a considerable influence upon business in a number of ways such as by providing financial support, imposing health and safety regulations, and by providing road and rail links.

Types of government

4. Liberal democracies. The liberal democracy is the most usual form of government in the free market or capitalist economies of the western world, and its essential feature is that power is vested in the people. Over many centuries people have gained various 'rights' such as of free speech and of freedom of the press, and these *civil rights* are the hallmark of a democratic form of government. The political system is based upon elections by which people elect representatives to rule over them.

5. Communism. About one-third of the peoples of the world live in communist states with command economies such as the USSR and China. The form of government is based upon the ideology of Karl Marx by which over a period of time all class distinctions will be removed and all property and goods held in common ownership. In most communist countries governments with dictatorial powers have emerged, usually as the result of revolution, and a single communist party dominates the political system. Other political parties and organizations are prohibited and the government makes all decisions affecting the running of the country.

6. Government in the Third World. The less-developed countries of the Third World exhibit a variety of governmental features. Many of them have developed from colonial regimes in which they were part of empires founded by countries such as Britain, Spain, and Portugal. Most former colonies have gained independence but in many cases are still developing their new forms of government. In many, constitutional forms of government have broken down and dictatorships – civil or military – have replaced them.

Government of the UK

7. The British Constitution. The rules which define the functions and powers of government are contained in a country's *constitution.*

Usually this is represented by a single document, such as in the USA and France, containing laws which are concerned with citizens' rights, elections, and powers of the executive. Britain, however, does not have a written constitution, but has instead an unwritten constitution based largely upon tradition and custom, as well as relevant laws from the past, even including such famous examples as the Magna Carta of 1215. This body of law is constantly being added to, for example, by the Representation of the People Act, 1969 by which the voting age was lowered to 18.

The main feature of the British Constitution is the unwritten practices which have developed over time and which ensure the smooth working of our government. These *conventions* ensure that modifications can be made to our system of government to meet needs as they arise, for example, it has become accepted practice for the Prime Minister to be a member of the House of Commons rather than the House of Lords.

The constitution of a state has to outline the powers and responsibilities of its three main functions:

(*a*) legislative (the making of law);
(*b*) executive (administering these laws); and
(*c*) judicial (judging laws).

It is accepted that these powers should be held by different bodies in order to ensure that the wishes of the people are not overruled by a government with too much power. In Britain the form of government is a compromise between allowing the government the authority to work effectively whilst at the same time making sure that the liberty of the individual is safeguarded. Whilst legislative powers (Parliament) and executive powers (Cabinet) are fused by the government being formed from Parliament, the independence of the judiciary is held to be vital in maintaining a check on the powers of the government.

8. The British system of government. Britain is a *monarchy*, and sovereignty – that is, the exercise of power – is vested in the Crown. Since the Glorious Revolution of 1688, however, it has been a *constitutional monarchy* in which powers are wielded, in the name of the ruling monarch, by a government which is democratically elected by the people. The Queen is Head of State and commands the loyalty and respect of the British people and the Commonwealth, while her executive powers are now in the hands of the government.

9. Parliament. Parliament is the supreme legislative authority in the land, and consists of the Queen, the House of Lords, and the House of Commons. The involvement of all three is needed for law-making, but they meet only on formal occasions such as the State opening of Parliament. In common with most other countries there are two chambers – Lords and Commons.

(*a*) The House of Lords is the upper chamber and although originally membership was hereditary, there are now a number of life peers. The House of Lords undertakes much of the legislative work of Parliament in addition to acting as the highest court of justice in the land, but its powers have been limited over the years.

(*b*) The House of Commons is the chamber within which the real power rests, as its Members of Parliament (MPs) are the elected representatives of the people of Britain. The government is formed from the members of the political party who obtain a majority of seats in a general election and who are able to command the support of the House.

10. Law-making. The making of laws is the function of Parliament, and requires the assent of the monarch. The various stages in legislation are as follows.

(*a*) The proposed new law will probably be part of the policy of the party forming the government, although influence may have been brought to bear by a pressure group or by the findings of a Royal Commission. New legislation may also appear as a Private Member's Bill submitted by an MP.

(*b*) It is usual to allow for a lengthy period of consultation with the public and with organizations concerned. To do this, the government of the day will often publish its proposals as a *White Paper* or possibly at an earlier stage as a *Green Paper* intended to promote public debate.

(*c*) The proposals are then formally drafted as a Bill.

(*d*) The Bill is then presented to the House of Commons for the formal *first reading*.

(*e*) The *second reading* is a more important stage at which the principles are debated, and the attendance of members would probably have been demanded by the party Whips.

(*f*) The Bill then proceeds to the *committee stage* for detailed examination and for any amendments thought necessary.

(*g*) The *report stage* then provides an opportunity for the whole House to suggest further amendments.

(*h*) The Bill proceeds to the *third reading* at which it can be either accepted or rejected by the House.

(*i*) At that point the Bill leaves the Commons for the House of Lords where it is reviewed. Bills must be passed by both Houses and can start in the House of Lords, where the same procedure is followed. The Lords can suggest changes and amendments (unless it is a Money Bill) but their powers are now limited to delaying legislation for a year.

(*j*) The Bill then goes to the monarch for the Royal Assent and then becomes law.

Because of the pressure on parliamentary time, the practice of *delegated legislation* has developed whereby Parliament passes laws granting outline powers to authorities such as local councils who then have the right to make *by-laws*.

The machinery of government

11. Elections. A General Election has to be held at least every five years, at which the people elect, by secret ballot, their representatives to sit in the House of Commons. Everyone over the age of 18, with some exceptions such as peers and lunatics, has the franchise, that is, the right to vote. A candidate for a seat in the House of Commons as a Member of Parliament (MP) has to be nominated for a constituency, usually by a political party. The main parties produce a manifesto in which they outline their legislative proposals, and the party which wins the election and forms the government is then said to have a mandate – the approval of the electorate to implement those proposals.

12. Forming a government. When the result of the General Election is known, the leader of the party obtaining a majority of the seats in the House of Commons is sent for by the Queen and invited to form a government. The leader firstly chooses 20 or so leading members of the party to form the Cabinet and then appoints other party members to less senior posts as members of the government (approximately 100 people). Once appointments have been approved by the monarch, the government becomes the policy-making body, making and implementing policy for the duration of that Parliament.

13. Opposition. The largest minority party forms the official Opposition and its leader appoints senior colleagues to the *Shadow Cabinet*. During the life of the Parliament the Opposition has the duty to criticise and oppose Government measures with which it is in disagreement, and to present itself to the public as an alternative government, ready to take office the moment it is needed.

14. Parliament. The life of the Parliament is divided into annual sessions, usually commencing in October or November. At the start of each session the Queen's Speech to Parliament outlines the government's legislative programme. The session then proceeds with government proposals debated in both Houses. Much of the work of Parliament is accomplished by committees. In the House of Commons, committees provide a vital opportunity for back-bench MPs to participate, either in standing committees examining bills or in select committees which examine the work of government departments.

15. Administration. The day-to-day administration of the country is carried out by the Civil Service. Civil Servants are appointed by the Crown, usually to government departments in which they are responsible to Ministers, who are in turn answerable to Parliament. The Civil Service is politically impartial, carrying out the policies of the elected government formed from any political party. Within the 30 or so government departments it is responsible for the whole range of public administration, and it is vital in ensuring continuity in government.

16. Participation and pressure. It is important in a democracy that the public, in addition to choosing a Government, should be able to participate in decision-making during the life of a Parliament. Unlike many other countries, a referendum, i.e. a direct vote by the people such as the decision to remain in the EC in 1975, is not an established practice in Britain. However, the voice of the people is heard through the activities of bodies known as *pressure groups*. Some of these organizations are permanent and their views sought by government, for example such professional associations as the Law Society. Others may be formed to oppose Government policy on current issues such as nuclear disarmament, for example, the Campaign for Nuclear Disarmament (CND). The depth of public feeling on certain issues may be gauged by the demonstrations, protest marches, and other measures taken.

Government and finance

17. Expenditure. The range of the state's activities and increasing expenditure has grown over many years, and extends from its original duties to maintain law and order to more recent responsibilities such as providing training facilities for workers. The right hand column in Fig. 2.1 shows how government expenditure is distributed. The costs of many services have increased considerably, for example with more sophisticated weapons and equipment for defence and more advanced medical care facilities.

18. Income. Increased state spending obviously means that more money has to be raised to finance the services provided. Public money is raised through the government presenting proposals – based on estimates by each department – to Parliament which then has to examine them and grant approval. The government's proposals for spending and raising revenue are presented in the Budget to Parliament by the Chancellor of the Exchequer in March or April. After examination by Parliament, the proposals are incorporated in the Finance Act by which formal permission for raising and spending money is granted. The responsibility for deciding upon financial matters rests exclusively with the House of Commons, although as the Government has a majority of supporters in favour of its proposals, the function of 'watchdog' of the nation's finances falls upon the Opposition. The left column of

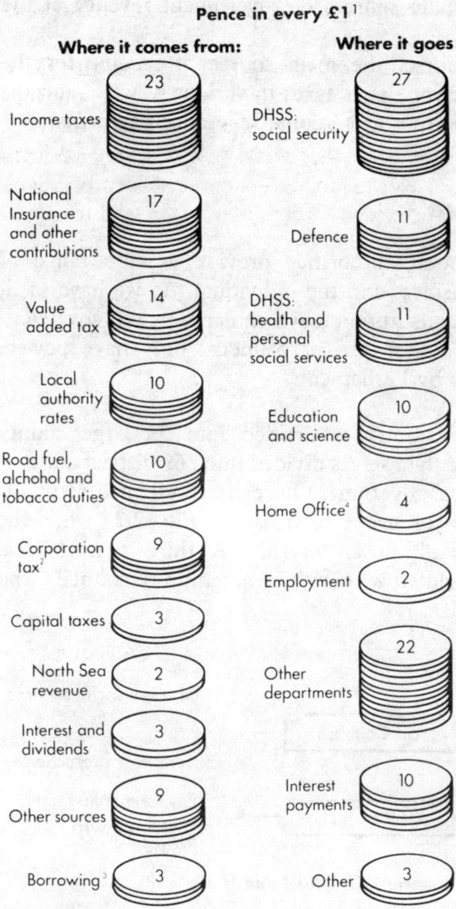

Cash totals of revenue and expenditure £173 billion

1 Rounded to nearest penny
2 Excluding North Sea
3 By central and local government
4 And Lord Chancellor's Department

Source: Derived from Financial Statement and Budget Report 1987-88. Table 1.2

Figure 2.1 *Government income and expenditure 1987–88*

Fig. 2.1 shows the main sources of government revenue at the present time.

Taxation is, of course, the main source of income for the government, and everyone pays taxes in various ways, as income tax, VAT on purchases, or as National Insurance payments.

Local government

19. Introduction. Local authorities provide a wide range of services, both for business and the individual. As we have seen, Britain has a unitary constitution in which Parliament is sovereign, and therefore local authorities (or councils) only have powers conferred upon them by Parliament.

20. Structure. The country is divided into 53 large county authorities, which are themselves divided into 369 district authorities. Both tiers of local government have clearly-defined responsibilities, the counties for major services (*see* Fig. 2.2) while the districts provide mainly local services. A third tier of local government is represented by parish or community councils who provide local amenities.

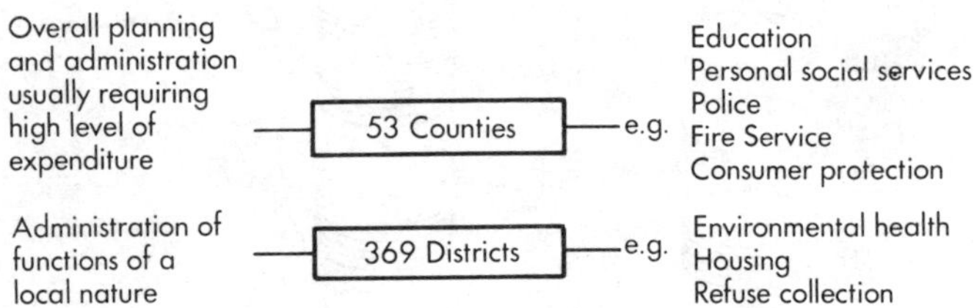

Figure 2.2 *Local Government in England and Wales*

21. Elections. Everyone over the age of 18 is entitled to vote in the council area in which he or she is resident. Local elections are normally held every four years. The elected councillors are unpaid but are normally entitled to claim expenses while on council business. A chairman is elected annually, and may have the title of Mayor or Lord Mayor if the authority is a borough or city.

22. Committees. Much of the work of local government is accomplished by committees which may have powers delegated to them by the full council. Financial matters such as rates or loans are, however, legally the duty of the full council and may not be delegated to a committee.

23. Financing local government. Expenditure by local authorities on services accounts for about a quarter of total public spending. The largest proportion – almost a third – is spent on education. Councils finance their spending by local rates (a tax on property soon to be replaced by the *community charge* or *poll tax* – *see* 5:**18**), and grants from central government. The main central government grant is the *rate support grant*, calculated to remedy differences between areas and to supplement local rates, but some services such as police receive special grants.

24. Services. Services are provided within a statutory framework and councils may have a legal obligation to provide certain of them. Expenditure on services has to be within this framework and may be sought by the council as an Act of Parliament, but any other spending would be *ultra vires*, (i.e. outside the law). The Audit Commission is an independent body which ensures that the accounts of local councils are audited satisfactorily and that economic use is made of their resources. The main services provided are shown in Fig. 2.2.

25. Local government and business. The wide range of services and the increase in expenditure by local councils in recent years has led to attempts by central government to restrict grants and the amount raised via rates. Local government expenditure is normally about 25 per cent of total public expenditure. As employers, councils employ 2.9 million people, more than the number employed by central government. Unlike the local government system in other countries, in Britain councils are not allowed a 'general competence' to set up business activities. The development of local enterprise agencies (LEAs), usually a partnership between public and private sector organizations as a form of local self-help, has proved a valuable stimulus to business development at the local level. LEAs are usually staffed by people seconded from local councils and large companies, and offer a range of services such as advice, training, and access to capital.

QUANGOS

Quasi autonomous non-governmental bodies have become a popular means of providing specialized functions in recent years. As many as one thousand organizations may be counted under this heading, such as Industrial Training Boards, tribunals, Marketing Boards, and the TC (Training Commission).

International government

26. Trends. In recent years there has been an inevitable trend towards groups of countries associating together to share certain responsibilities such as defence or for economic co-operation and development.

27. The European Community (EC). The EC was established (as the European Economic Community, EEC) in 1957 between six Western European powers – West Germany, France, The Netherlands, Belgium, Italy, and Luxembourg. Britain joined in 1973 and membership now includes twelve nations. The objective of the Community is to extend economic cooperation between its members in order to achieve a common market for trade by removing barriers between them. With the removal of barriers, a closer union is expected and the possibility of the emergence of Europe as a single political unit.

The EEC operates through its own institutional structure (*see* Fig. 2.3), establishing laws which become binding upon member nations. Policies are proposed by the European Commission, based in Brussels, and decisions are made by the Council of Ministers, the executive body consisting of one representative of each member country. The European Parliament has members elected to it from all member countries, and the European Court of Justice ensures laws are kept.

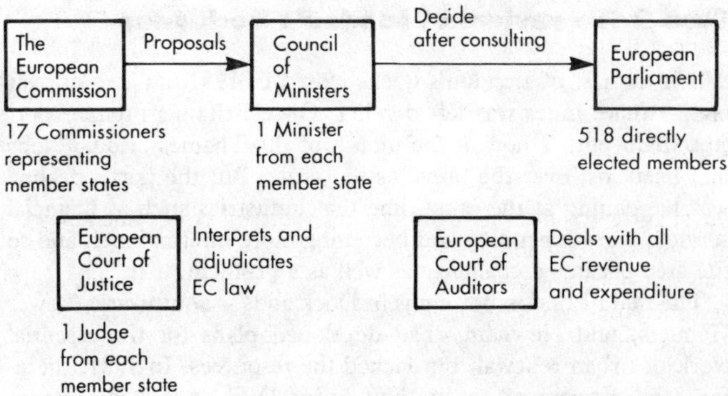

Figure 2.3 *The European Community at work*

Business in Britain is affected by Community laws and directives, for example regulating how products are to be measured or decribed (*see* 3: **Case 3**). Subsidies to the European fund are paid by each country, and from it grants are made for business and industry in those countries which are in need. Loan capital may be obtained from the European Investment Bank, while the Regional Development Fund provides grants for development of regions requiring aid. The Social Fund provides funds for retraining labour and for resettlement of workers forced to move jobs.

28. International organizations. A number of economic agencies of UNO (the United Nations Organization) aid international business.

(*a*) *IMF.* The IMF (International Monetary Fund) was established in 1944 to encourage stability in international trade. Payments are made by countries into a fund from which countries may borrow when facing short-term trading difficulties.

(*b*) *The World Bank* (International Bank for Reconstruction and Development). This exists to lend money to nations in need, especially the less-developed countries of the Third World.

(*c*) *GATT.* The GATT (General Agreement on Tariffs and Trade) was established in 1948 to encourage free trade between nations by the removal of tariffs and quotas whenever possible.

Case 2 The revival of London's Docklands

When the last of London's docks closed in 1981, an area of over eight square miles was left derelict. Once Britain's premier port (the main port is now at the mouth of the Thames), 20,000 jobs had been lost over the previous ten years. But the port's decline was happening at the same time that industries such as financial services were expanding and becoming more international, and so the area became a challenge as well as a problem.

The main London boroughs in Docklands – Southwark, Tower Hamlets, and Newham – had developed plans for the essential work of urban renewal, but lacked the resources. In 1981, therefore, the government set up the London Docklands Development Corporation (LDDC) – a QUANGO – as the planning authority for the area with powers to buy and sell land, demolish buildings, and improve the infrastructure. The LDDC has public money for its work of urban renewal but also has the power to form partnerships with private sector organizations which undertake most of the development work such as building office blocks and housing accommodation.

The pace of development has been brisk. Communications have been seen as a priority, and the Docklands Light Railway was built as a basis for quicker travel for commuters, while the London City Airport (less than six miles from the Bank of England) offers considerable potential for international business links. The expansion of the financial services industry has seen firms moving from the City into purpose-built office complexes in Docklands, and a number of major newspapers are now produced there rather than in Fleet Street.

Reaction by the residents of Docklands has not, however, been generally appreciative. Most of the housing in the area is rented from local councils, but the nearness to London has seen an inevitable development of more highly-priced accommodation sought after by workers in financial services in the City. There are a number of local pressure groups representing the community spirit of the East End and the Docklands Forum was formed to express their views and challenge decisions. The LDDC has now established Skillnet, as its own training and education service, and further initiatives are, it is hoped, encouraging people to acquire the skills needed by the new industries.

Progress test 2

1. What is government? (**1**)
2. Why is it important to business? (**2**)
3. What are the main world types of government? (**3-5**)
4. Briefly describe the British Constitution. (**6**)
5. How are laws made? (**10**)
6. How is a government formed? (**12**)
7. What is the role of the Civil Service? (**15**)
8. What is a Pressure Group? (**16**)
9. What are the government's main items of expenditure? (**17**)
10. How does it raise money? (**17**)
11. How important is local government to business? (**25**)
12. What is the EC? Explain how it works. (**27**)
13. Describe the role of:- (a) IMF, (b) GATT, and (c) World Bank. (**28**)
14. What is a QUANGO? Explain the role of the LDDC. (**Case 2**)
15. How did public and private sectors co-operate in the renewal of London Docklands? (**Case 2**)
16. How did residents of Docklands express their views? (**Case 2**)

3

The legal framework

Introduction

1. Definition. Law can be defined as being a set of rules which regulate human conduct and which is imposed by the State. There may be many rules which govern aspects of behaviour in society, for example, rules of morality which dictate our standards of honesty, or conventions which determine a fashionable way of dressing, but it is important to ensure that what we understand as 'law' is distinguished from such rules as these. Law:

(*a*) is part of a country's body of legislation which applies to all its citizens; and
(*b*) is enforced by that country's sovereign body.

We speak therefore of law as having binding force upon the citizens of a country, and breaking of the law is punishable by sanctions. Law is an essential feature of all advanced societies, ensuring the harmonious relationship of people, organizations, and government. Business is subject to the law as all citizens and organizations are, whilst there are also many aspects of law which are specific to business matters, for example, relating to finance, company organization, and consumer affairs.

Sources of law

2. Statutes. The basis of most countries' law is legislation passed by the sovereign body. The policies of the government are presented to the legislature and, when approved, become law. In

Britain, the constitutional position is that the sovereign body is the Queen-in-Parliament, and statutes enacted by Parliament and approved by the sovereign become part of the law of the land (*see* 2:**10**). Whilst statutory law is not a major source of English law, it is an important means by which defects can be remedied and changes made, for example, for social or economic reasons.

Once a law has been made, courts have to apply its provisions, despite any misgivings judges may have about it. The *Separation of Powers* is an important feature of the British Constitution whereby Parliament does not intervene in the judicial process and judges will likewise not criticize nor interfere in the laws they have to apply. Judges will, however, have to interpret laws in every case they try and it is therefore possible that application of a law in some cases will not fulfil the intentions of the legislature. In order to ensure that the exact meaning of a law is applied, certain *rules of interpretation* have been developed over the years to assist judges.

Delegated legislation, by which other bodies are granted authority by Parliament to make laws, has become an important aspect of law. This has been made necessary by the increasing pressure of time upon Parliament and the technical nature of many aspects of legislation, for example, as in building regulations. Delegated (or subordinate) legislation may take the following forms.

(*a*) Statutory Instruments (SI), by which the general principles of legislation may be outlined by Parliament (for example, concerning safety standards or health requirments), and the powers to establish rules within this framework granted to other bodies. This is frequently the means whereby aspects of law involving business are made by government departments such as the Ministry of Transport.

(*b*) Orders in Council are those made by the monarch and Privy Council under authority delegated by Parliament.

(*c*) By-laws, usually made by a local authority, but also by other bodies such as public corporations. By-laws have to be confirmed by a government minister and usually provide for local conditions, such as local trading hours or traffic control.

3. Common law. The basis of British law is the *unwritten* or *common* law that has survived for centuries. For many years after the Norman Conquest of 1066 justice depended upon itinerant judges who visited towns throughout the land on 'circuits' to hear cases. Initially they administered the customs of each locality they visited, but gradually these customs became unified into a body of law which we refer to as the common law, that is, 'common' to the whole country.

4. Custom. Although local customs were important in providing a basis for the development of common law, they are not today of significance. Custom may only be of importance in such issues as a right of way which may be resolved by establishing the length of time a right may have existed.

5. Equity. As common law became established as a rigid body of law, gaps inevitably appeared. Many disputes needed honest and impartial examination of individual circumstances and were referred to the Lord Chancellor who sought fairness and equity in all decisions. Equity therefore became an important source of law, especially in matters of conscience, for example, an injunction may be obtained from a court to restrain a person continuing a nuisance.

6. Case law. As we have seen, judges were instrumental in developing common law. Judgements are made by reference to past cases on the principle of *judicial precedent*, and thus over the years a body of judge-made or case law has developed. Case law is regarded with suspicion as it leads to uncertainty over the outcome of a case which may depend upon a judge's interpretation of past cases.

7. Law merchant. Law developed in the early days of Britain's trade with other countries is known as *law merchant*. Foreign traders brought different laws and customs with them and special courts were frequently convened to try commercial cases. They were slowly absorbed into the general body of law although many basic principles of law applying to business today are derived from early trade practices.

8. EC law. All member countries of the European Community are subject to legislation made by the Community. With the enlargement of the Community an increasing volume of legislation has resulted, which takes precedence over the national laws of countries as long as they remain members. The emphasis of the EC upon economic integration means that much of the legislation is of considerable importance to business, for example, law governing trade descriptions. The Council of Ministers and the Commission can make:

(*a*) *regulations*, which are law and are therefore binding upon all member states,
(*b*) *directives*, which require member countries to pass legislation to bring them into force; and
(*c*) decisions, which are usually specific to a certain organization or firm.

The European Court of Justice in Luxembourg, interprets EC law and is responsible for ensuring that member states implement Community decisions. Appeals regarding Community law or its application can be made to the Court by member states, individuals, or firms.

9. International law. The principles of international law may be accepted as being part of a country's body of law, and may be significant for business, for example, in such matters as transport or fishing rights.

Classification of law

10. Public and private law. It is usual to distinquish between *public law* in which crimes are committed against the state and society, and *private law* which governs the relationship between people, firms, and organizations. In Britain, the procedures by which cases within criminal law and civil law are tried are organized separately.

11. Criminal law. Criminal proceedings may be taken for offences against the state (e.g. treason), against the person (e.g. murder), or against property (e.g. theft, fraud). Prosecutions are brought by the police and cases are generally heard in open court by the accusatorial system, that is, defence and prosecution cases are presented and cross-examined, with a judge acting as umpire.

Criminal cases may be heard in Magistrates' Courts, Crown Courts, or Courts of Appeal.

(*a*) *Magistrates' Courts*, where they are tried by justices of the peace. JPs are members of the public who are unpaid and unqualified, assisted by a legally qualified clerk. Two or three magistrates usually sit together – the *Bench* – and deal with a variety of cases. Cases may be either a *summary trial* of lesser offences for which magistrates are empowered to convict and sentence (up to six months imprisonment and fine up to £2,000), or *committal proceedings* in which they examine a case before referring it to a higher court. Magistrates Courts are a vital part of thelegal system of the country by virtue of their heavy workload, disposing of about 95 per cent of criminal cases in England and Wales.

(*b*) *Crown Courts* try the more serious cases. Cases are heard before a judge, and the accused can elect for trial by jury.

(*c*) *Courts of Appeal*. Appeals against sentence or conviction may be made to the Court of Appeal or to the House of Lords, the highest court of justice in the land.

12. Civil law. Civil cases vary widely in nature, and concern the rights and duties of individuals and organizations to one another, for example, in matters affecting contract or property. Whereas criminal justice is intended to punish where necessary, civil justice seeks redress or compensation for wrongs which may have been committed.

Civil cases may be heard in County Courts, the High Court, Courts of Appeal, or Restrictive Practices Court.

(*a*) *County Courts*. Cases are heard before a judge who is able to deal with a variety of offences within specified limits, for example, involving relatively small amounts of money. Divorce, adoption, disputes involving rent legislation, and claims under credit agreements are typical of the work of the County Court.

(*b*) *The High Court* deals with more serious cases. It is divided into three divisions:

(*i*) the Queen's Bench Division which deals with such matters as a breach of contract or claim for damages, (*ii*) the Chancery Division which hears cases in company matters, bankruptcy, and taxation; and

(*iii*) the Family Division which is concerned with such domestic matters as divorce and property disputes.

(*c*) *Courts of Appeal.* (As for criminal cases in 11c above.)

(*d*) *Restrictive Practices Courts.* Cases are referred by the Registrar of Restrictive Practices. If an agreement is felt by the Registrar to fail to comply to the code governing restrictive practices, it can be heard in the Court before a judge and two lay assessors.

13. Legal aid. To assist people of limited financial means involved in legal action, state support in the form of legal aid is available. Candidates have to show that their financial state satisfies the criteria for aid, and if so they can choose a solicitor and continue with the proceedings.

Legal personality

14. Definition. A legal person is one recognized by law as having rights and duties. However, law distinquishes between a 'natural' person, that is a single human being, and an 'artificial' person formed by an association of people, such as a company or club, which then has a single legal personality.

15. Natural persons. Every human being is a legal person from the moment of birth until death. But one person's status may differ from that of another for example, nationality may confer the rights and duties of a country only upon its citizens, while diplomatic immunity might mean that diplomats of a foreign country are not subject to the laws of a country in which they work. People below the age of 18 are known in law as *minors* and are subject to special rules in law relating, for instance, to responsibilities in contracts, or ownership of land. Similarly, special provisions may also exist for people suffering from mental disorders, for bankrupts, and for non-nationals.

16. Corporations. A corporation is formed by a number of people who associate together for a common purpose and which is then regarded in law as a single legal person. Once formed, a corporation can then enter into contracts, buy and sell land, and act as a single, independent entity. A corporation may be:

(*a*) a *corporation sole* consisting of only one member, usually an official post held by different people in succession, such as the Crown; *or*

(*b*) a *corporation aggregate* which consists of a number of members at the same time. This is a far more usual form of organization and the corporation has a legal personality distinct from those of its members. This means that members can enter into a legal relationship with it, for example make contracts with it or take legal action against it. A corporation aggregate may be formed in one of three ways:

(*i*) by Royal Charter, such as the BBC, universities.

(*ii*) by Act of Parliament, for example, the boards of nationalised industries.

(*iii*) by registration as a company according to the provisions of the Companies Act, 1985 (*see* 4:7).

17. Unincorporated associations. A number of organizations exist which are formed by a group of people but which are not incorporated, and are not treated in law as a single person. It is most usual for this to be the form of organization for such bodies as sports and social clubs and societies of various types. Because such associations do not have a separate legal identity, legal actions taken are the collective responsibility of all members. Trustees may be appointed to be responsible on behalf of members for such duties as ownership of property, and committees may be formed to undertake certain responsibilities. The most important unincorporated associations are partnerships and trade unions.

(*a*) Partnerships are business associations regulated by the Partnership Act, 1890. A partnership does not have a separate legal existence, and all partners are equally liable in law for business dealings undertaken. The formation of a limited partnership in which one partner is an unlimited general partner while others may be limited to the amount of their stake in the firm was made possible by the Limited Partnerships Act, 1907. (*see* 4:5).

(*b*) Trade unions are unincorporated associations, usually of employees who have formed an association to protect their conditions of work.

Personnel of the law

18. Solicitors. Most solicitors work in partnerships and have been 'admitted' by the Law Society by serving a period of time articled to a practising solicitor. A wide range of work is undertaken, such as conveyancing (buying and selling property), and probate (resolving details of a will).

19. Barristers. Barristers are members of one of the Inns of Court and upon qualification are 'called to the bar'. They are briefed by solicitors to take cases in courts on behalf of clients and usually specialize in a specific aspect of law.

20. Legal executives. Much of the routine legal work, especially in solicitors' offices is performed by qualified legal executives.

21. Judges. Judges are appointed by the Crown from the ranks of experienced barristers. They are independent of political powers and have immunity in law from statements made in court.

22. Jurors. The jury system is a traditional feature of British law. Juries in the High Court consist of twelve people chosen from the electoral roll, and service is compulsory. The function of the jury is to produce a verdict on the question of fact put to them by the judge.

Law and business

23. Influence of the law upon business. Law is an important aspect of all forms of business activity. Whilst all business organizations are subject to the general body of law in the same way as individuals, certain aspects of law have a direct influence and effect upon business.

24. Law of contract. The law of contract is the foundation of much of commercial law. A contract is an agreement which is intended by the parties entering into it to confer rights and impose obligations which will be enforceable by law. An agreement has to satisfy six main requirements before it can be accepted as being a legally binding contract:

(*a*) There must have been a definite *offer* by one party, for example to make a purchase at a certain price, and a clear *acceptance* of that offer by another party.

(*b*) The parties to the contract must have a clear *intention* to create a legal relationship, and a penalty may have to be paid if a contract is not completed.

(*c*) Unless made under seal, a contract must be supported by *consideration*, that is, each party must fulfil a promise or suffer some loss as, for example, the payment of a sum of money in return for a service rendered.

(*d*) The parties to the contract must have legal *capacity*, that is, minors or people suffering from mental disorders cannot enter into a contract.

(*e*) The consent of the parties to the contract must be *genuine*, that is, there must be no mistake regarding details, fraud, nor any undue influence brought to bear.

(*f*) The contract must be *legal*, and cannot be enforced if itinvolves, for example, a restrictive trade practice or misleading trades description.

A contract which does not satisfy any one of the above requirements may be void or voidable:

(*a*) a contract which is declared void does not exist, as it will not be recognized by the courts;

(*b*) a contract which is voidable can be avoided by one of the parties, for example, a minor who does not have the capacity to enter into a contract.

When the duties undertaken by a contract come to an end, so then do the rights, and the contract is said to be *discharged*. Discharge may take place in a variety of ways:-

(*a*) *by performance*, that is, the obligations imposed by the contract will be carried out and concluded;

(*b*) *by agreement*, whereby the parties, having agreed to the contract can subsequently agree to bring it to an end;

(*c*) *by lapse of time*, if a specific period of time is agreed in the contract, as in a short-term contract of employment;

(*d*) *by frustration*, caused by circumstances which prevent the fulfilment of the conditions, such as when an injured employee becomes unable to continue in employment;

(*e*) *by breach of contract*, by which one party fails to deliver goods or refuses to perform a service. The usual remedy available to the injured party is an action for damages which compensate for loss occurred as a result of the failure to complete the conditions of the contract.

25. Law of tort. A tort is a civil wrong which may give rise to legal proceedings as a result of a breach of duty. A variety of torts exist in which a person may be in a position of having a duty or liability to others, and failure to carry out that duty might result in damage to them. In some cases one person may be responsible for the torts of another, for example, the principle of *vicarious liability* which rules that an employer may be responsible for damage caused by one of his or her employees in the course of employment. Some of the most important torts are negligence, nuisance, and defamation.

(*a*) *Negligence*, where a person has omitted to do something which a 'reasonable' person would have been expected to do. In the case of *Donoghue* v. *Stevenson* the manufacturer of a bottle of ginger beer which had been found to contain a snail was ruled to have been negligent as the company had a duty of care to consumers.

(*b*) *Nuisance*. A *public* nuisance is caused to the public at large, for example, an obstruction of a pavement, while a *private* nuisance might be interference with someone's use of land, such as unpleasant smells experienced by living close to a factory.

(*c*) *Defamation*, by which false statements may damage a person's reputation: by *libel*, that is in permanent form such as in writing or on radio or television; or by *slander*, usually held to be spoken.

26. Law of employment. The general principles of the law of contract (*see* **24**) apply to the formation of a contract of employment. *See* Chapter 12 for specific details of employment.

27. Consumer law. The government's acceptance of the need to ensure protection of consumers has produced a range of varied legislation dealing with both criminal and civil offences. See Chapter 16 for details of consumer protection.

Administrative justice

28. Administrative law. Administrative law is concerned with the organization and procedures of public authorities and the ways in which they are controlled. The increasing volume of social legislation, for example, in education, health, and housing, has brought the citizen into close relationship with government bodies and made it necessary to ensure that individual rights are respected and disputes resolved. The difficulties which arise are mainly a result of administrative errors, for example, in the payment of pensions or welfare benefits, and whilst disputes can be dealt with by courts of law, a number of alternative arrangements have been created to resolve problems more speedily and cheaply. The main means whereby the citizen may seek administrative justice are as follows.

(*a*) *Administrative Tribunals.* Administrative Tribunals have become the main form by which justice may be sought outside of the main courts for many routine administrative disputes. Many tribunals are permanent, dealing with regularly occurring disputes in such fields as employment, (e.g. unfair dismissal), land (e.g. compensation for compulsory purchase), or social security (e.g. industrial injuries). Tribunals offer a means whereby disagreement may be resolved swiftly by people who are experts in a particular field, but are sometimes criticized because decisions are discretionary and reasons not always given. Some professional bodies have their own machinery empowered to determine matters of discipline within a profession, for example, the Law Society and the General Medical Council.

(*b*) *Parliamentary Commissioner for Administration.* The office of Parliamentary Commissioner for Administration (Ombudsman) was established to investigate complaints of maladministration by the public. A complaint has to be made via a Member of Parliament, and the Commissioner has to report findings to

Parliament. Typically, the nature of a complaint is one arising from delay, neglect, or bias in a decision made by a government department, and is remedied as the result of recommendations made by the Commissioner. Health Service Commissioners and Local Commissioners have been set up to deal with the more specialized nature of complaints arising within the health service and in local government.

(*c*) *Arbitration*. In some cases the most convenient means of settling a dispute may be by arbitration rather than by the law courts. This is often the case where both parties to a dispute may agree to arbitration when a compromise solution is possible, for example, in settlement of a national wage dispute (*see* **Chap. 15**).

(*d*) *Statutory Enquiries*. In a number of instances, for example, compulsory purchase of land or complaints of pollution, a government minister has powers to examine evidence and to set up a local enquiry. Recommendations are made to the minister who will then issue a decision.

(*e*) *Royal Commissions*. On general matters involving various aspects of public services, a Royal Commission may be set up to make recommendations for changes. Evidence is collected from a wide variety of sources and the report is seen as an indication of how individual interests may best be served.

Case 3 European decisions and trading standards

An important aspect of European Community policy is that of consumer protection, and decisions made have an impact upon consumers in the UK. In 1976 a Directive (76/211/EEC) was passed by the Council of the European Community, concerning quality control for pre-packaged products. As an EC Directive, it then had to be implemented by the legislatures of the member states.

In Britain, a committee was set up to report upon its implementation, and the report was presented to Parliament as a White Paper (Cmnd 6805) in June, 1977. For Britain it meant a change from a system whereby minimum quantities were specified by law for many products, to a new system of average weights and quantities. Thus existing legislation in Britain had to be amended by the passing of the Weights and Measures Act, 1979, which brought the new system set out in the EC Directive into force.

The result is that for many products on sale in Britain, including foodstuffs such as beans and jams and liquids such as coffee and beer, the legal requirement is now based upon an agreed average for weight or volume as set out by the European Community.

Progress test 3

1. What is a law? (**1**)
2. What are the main sources of English law? (**2-9**)
3. What are the main forms of delegated legislation? (**2**)
4. What do you understand by (*a*) Common Law, and (*b*) Equity? (**3, 5**)
5. What is the importance of case law? (**6**)
6. Explain the nature of legislation in the EC. (**8**)
7. Distinquish between public law and private law.(**10**)
8. Describe (*a*) how a criminal case is tried, and (*b*) a civil case. (**11,12**)
9. What is legal aid? (**13**)
10. What do you understand by legal personality? (**14**)
11. Distinquish between corporations and unincorporated associations. (**16,17**)
12. What are the requirements of a valid contract? (**24**)
13. What is a tort? (**25**)
14. How can a citizen obtain administrative justice? (**28**)
15. What is the role of the Parliamentary Commisioner for Administration? (**28**)
16. How important is EC law for the UK and other member states? (**Case 3**)

Part two

Structure and organization of business

4

Forms of business organization

Introduction

1. Public and private sectors. There are a number of different forms of business organization and ownership. They can broadly be divided into those which are in the *private sector*, i.e. in the control of private individuals, and those in the *public sector*, i.e. owned by the government. Generally, the types of organization which exist are those which best serve the needs of the various business activities, and may be determined by such factors as scale, market, or resources. Many countries, including the UK, now have a mixed economy in which business activities take place in both the public sector and private sector.

The private sector

2. Definition. In the private sector there is a large number of small organizations such as the *sole proprietor, partnership,* and *company,* and also a smaller number of much larger companies and multinational corporations. Co-operative enterprises are increasing in number, and there are an increasing number of *buyouts* by management or staff of a firm who raise capital to take it over. In Britain, the private sector produces about 75 per cent of GDP, mainly in manufacturing industries, distributive trades, and the service sector. Firms in the private sector are profit-motivated and produce goods and service in response to market demand.

3. Sole proprietor. The single person firm is the original and simplest form of business undertaking, although the sole owner may, of course, employ others. The business is owned and operated by one person and there is no distinction between that person and the business organization. The owner provides the capital and takes the profits, and is completely responsible for all liabilities. It is a form of business most common in the service sector, and is typically a small newsagent's shop or a tradesman's business such as plumbing or decorating.

The advantages of this form of organization are that:

(*a*) it is simple and easy to establish, and to dissolve;
(*b*) there are few legal requirements, other than the possibility that a licence is necessary for some activities and that the Registrar of Business Names must be notified if the name of the business differs from its owners;
(*c*) customers receive personal attention;
(*d*) the owner has complete flexibility of management and control;
(*e*) profits are retained by the owner.

The disadvantages of sole proprietor businesses are that:

(*a*) the owner has unlimited liability for business debts, which could result in loss of personal possessions such as house and car;
(*b*) difficulties can arise, because of its small scale, in raising finance;
(*c*) expansion may be limited by managerial deficiencies;
(*d*) there is a high level of personal commitment involved in working long hours, often without holidays;
(*e*) lack of continuity of the business may result from the sickness, death, or bankruptcy of the owner.
(*f*) essential costs, for example, to satisfy safety, health. or hygiene regulations, become relatively higher for a small business;
(*g*) the smaller business is more vulnerable to competition.

Partnership

4. Introduction. The Partnership Act, 1890 made it possible for between two and 20 people to enter into co-ownership when more capital has to be raised for expansion of the business. Typically, there tend to be four or five people in a partnership, but in banking a maximum of ten partners is allowed, while accountants and solicitors may have in excess of 20. Partners have equal responsibilities and share profits and losses.

Partnerships are a form of business most commonly found in professions such as medicine, dentistry, law, accountancy, and estate agency, and also in professional services such as plumbing and building. Partnerships are frequently old family businesses, such as farms, which have been in a family for generations.

The advantages of the partnership as a form of organization are that:

(*a*) it enables the workload to be spread, for example during holiday time or in periods of illness.

(*b*) it allows for the development of specialization and the spread of expertise, ideas, experience, and management skills;

(*c*) there is access to more finance;

(*d*) continuity of the business is assured and partners may progress from junior to full partners;

(*e*) it is simple to establish as formal agreement is not necessary;

The disadvantages, on the other hand, are that:

(*a*) all partners have unlimited liability for the debts of the business;

(*b*) the business does not have a separate legal existence;

(*c*) conflict and disagreement between partners are possible;

(*d*) there is a risk of dissolution of the business, for example through the death or bankruptcy of a partner causing loss of capital.

5. Limited partnerships. The disadvantages listed above led to the Partnership Act, 1907 which sought to overcome the problem of unlimited liability by allowing 'sleeping' partners liable only for the amount of their investment. These partners cannot, however, be involved in the operation of the business, and one partner has to undertake unlimited liability. The limited partnership has lost popularity as it has become easier to form a company.

Companies

6. Definition. A company is a form of business organization which has been *incorporated,* i.e. it has been registered with the Registrar of Companies as a body which has an existence of its own, separate from that of its owners. The continuing expansion of business activity during the years of the Industrial Revolution created a demand for more capital, and the introduction of the principle of limited liability in 1855 provided encouragement for investment. Risks in investment could now be limited to only the amount of the investment made, and not the investor's whole estate, as was previously the case. Thus more capital became available and with it the demand for larger forms of business to utilize the capital more effectively.

7. Organization. A company is owned by its shareholders who appoint directors to control its operation. Funds are raised by shares in the form of small amounts bought by a number of small investors, and by large blocks of shares owned by organizations such as pension trusts and insurance companies. Companies have to conform to the conditions of trading laid down by successive Companies Acts, now consolidated in the Companies Act, 1985 which sets down requirements such as capital structure, rights and duties of directors, and preparation of accounts.

8. Forming a company. The procedure for setting up or 'floating' a new company is outlined below.

(*a*) The *Memorandum of Association,* stating the name of the company, its objectives, capital, and nature of the business, must be provided to the Registrar of Companies.

(*b*) This has to be accompanied by the *Articles of Association* which describe the organization and management of the company.

(*c*) The Registrar will issue a *Certificate of Incorporation* which gives the new firm legal personality, and at this point a private company (*see* **10**) can commence trading.

(d) Finally, the public company has to obtain a Certificate of Trading, confirming that shares have been offered for sale to the public, before the company can commence in business.

9. Dissolution of a company. As a company is created by law, its

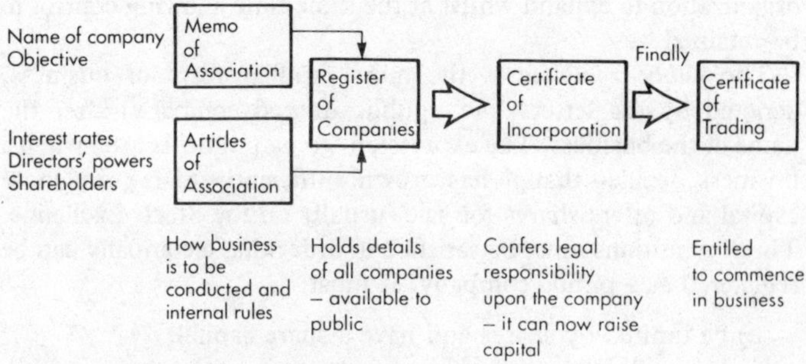

Figure 4.1 *How a limited company is formed*

existence can also be ended by law if, for example, financial difficulties are encountered. Dissolution of the company can take place in the following ways.

(*a*) *Compulsory liquidation*, by which a company which has become insolvent will be wound-up by order of a court of law. The court will appoint an Official Receiver to sell off the company's assets and pay debts.

(*b*) *Voluntary liquidation*, by which the company itself agrees to go into liquidation. It is possible in this case also that a court may decide to supervise liquidation.

10. Types of company. Companies vary considerably in size and type. Many companies have developed into multi-national corporations such as Ford, Dunlop, and ITT, while others develop a diversity of business interests as 'conglomerates', for example, the Rank Organisation. Companies which gain control of 51 per cent of the voting shares of another company are known as *holding companies.*

All companies are privately owned by their shareholders, but can be of two types – public companies and private companies.

The *private company*, established by the Companies Act, 1907, can have from two to an unlimited number of shareholders, and must have 'Limited' or 'Ltd' in its name. Shares can only be sold privately and are not available to the general public, and a private company can impose restrictions upon share transfer. This form of company caters mainly for the small family business and allows the organization to expand whilst at the same time allowing control to be retained.

The *public company* is the more familiar form of business, denoted by the letters 'plc' (public limited company) after the name of the business. The expression 'going public' is used when a business decides that it has grown sufficiently to require more capital and offers shares for sale, usually on the Stock Exchange. Three conditions must be satisfied in order that a company can be registered as a public company. It must:

(*a*) be limited by shares and have a share capital;
(*b*) have minimum specified capital requirements;
(*c*) be described as a plc in its articles of association.

The main advantages of the public company as a form of business are that:

(*a*) it has a separate legal existence, with rights in law;
(*b*) finance is more easily obtainable than in a private company, from large and small investors;
(*c*) continuity of existence is more likely because of the company's separate legal identity and by its wide spread of capital;
(*d*) limited liability safeguards investors and encourages investment.

The disadvantages can be said to be:

(*a*) the requirement, by the Registrar of Companies, of public disclosure and inspection of trading accounts;
(*b*) the legal formalities involved in setting up the business;
(*c*) that diseconomies of scale, such as remoteness, slow decision making, and lack of incentive, may appear with the growth of the company;
(*d*) that the divorce between ownership and management may become a problem;
(*e*) liability to takeovers by changes in share ownership.

Franchising

11. Introduction. Franchising is a form of business in which a product or service may be provided by people or firms who have obtained a licence from the originators or owners of that product or service. A franchise agreement is drawn up in which the rights of both parties are set down.

The parties to the agreement are:

(*a*) the *franchisor* – usually the person or firm who develops a new product or service – who decides to allow others to provide the product or service under licence;

(*b*) the *franchisee* – the person or firm who buys the licence granting the right to provide the product or service.

The franchisor usually owns a well-developed and reputable product or service, recognizable to the public under its trade name. The franchisor will have tried the product out by piloting it for a reasonable trading period before selling it to potential franchisees. The franchisee is provided with a total package for marketing the product, including, for example, the product's name and logo, any patented processes, accounting procedures, marketing strategy, and training services. The franchisee in return has to raise capital to pay the franchise fee, find suitable premises, equip them according to the franchisor's house-style, buy or lease equipment, and market the product to the standard specified by the franchisor. The franchisee is not employed by the franchising company, but has to establish and operate his or her own business, possibly as a self-employed person, in partnership with others, or as a company. It is usual for fees to be paid to the franchisor throughout the term of the franchise, usually as a royalty, for example, a fixed percentage (typically ten per cent) of weekly takings.

12. Development. Franchising is a well-established form of business in the USA where it accounts for 30 per cent of retail sales. In the UK it has never achieved the same popularity but recent years have seen considerable development.

One of the first franchises in Britain was Wimpy Bars, which opened in the late 1950s and now has many hundreds of outlets throughout the country. Other fast-food chains have also developed by franchising, such as Kentucky Fried Chicken and Spud-U-Like, based upon secret formulae and ingredients for preparation of standard product lines. Many of these franchises are expensive as purchase or lease of premises and equipment are necessary. Franchises which provide services may be less expensive, such as those providing various forms of cleaning and maintenance like Dyno-rod which provides a drain-clearing operation. Other popular services are word-processing, such as Prontaprint. Some franchises may simply be one person providing a single service, for example, 'job franchises' such as Home Tune which needs only one operative and a van to provide car maintenance and repair at customers' homes.

13. Advantages. For the franchisor, franchising provides the opportunity of developing the business without having to incur large capital sums.

For the franchisee it:

(*a*) enables people to go into business with limited risk and outlay;
(*b*) ensures that the product or service has been thoroughly tested and marketed before the franchise has been approved;
(*c*) provides a well-known brand name and image, and large-scale advertising back-up;
(*d*) requires less capital than other forms of business start-up;
(*e*) provides continuing back-up support and advice during the period of the franchise agreement.

14. Disadvantages.

(*a*) The franchisee may resent the amount of control exercised by the franchisor.
(*b*) Loss of motivation may occur by depending too heavily upon the franchisor.
(*c*) In some cases the support provided by the franchisor has been inadequate.

15. The British Franchise Association. This is the trade association for franchising companies. It was established in 1977 to promote ethical standards for the industry, and its member firms have to abide by its code of ethics designed to protect franchisees. It provides an advisory service for prospective franchisees.

Co-operatives

16. Definition. Co-operative ownership is a form of business organization in which there is a voluntary association of people to operate an enterprise collectively. Although placed within the private sector, co-operatives differ in some respects from other institutions in that their aim is not mainly profit-making.

17. Development. The co-operative movement has a long history in Britain, the first shop being set up in Toad Lane, Rochdale in 1844 by some weavers who decided to provide an alternative to the 'truck shops' of the mill owners. They subscribed £1 each, shared out food among themselves which they bought in bulk, and paid out the surplus money remaining to themselves as a dividend. The self-help movement of the times persisted in the form of building societies, mutual insurance companies such as Scottish Widows, and the Co-operative Bank, while the Co-operative Party was formed in 1917 to further the political aim of the movement.

18. Organization. There have been many developments in co-operative organization since its establishment, but the democratic principle, with each member having one vote in running affairs, remains the same. The original form of organization was as Friendly Societies, not covered within the Companies Acts. Today, however, many organizations based upon co-operative principles have become corporate bodies with full legal powers, for example, building societies following the Building Societies Act 1985.

The advantages of co-operative ownership include:

(*a*) the ideal of providing quality goods at a reasonable price;
(*b*) members share in the profits;
(*c*) democratic control of the enterprise by workers and members;
(*d*) many benefits are provided for members;
(*e*) there is less likelihood of business activities being sold off.

The disadvantages tend to be that:

(*a*) the local and small-scale nature of most co-operatives has impeded the development and benefits of large-scale operation;

(*b*) co-operatives are vulnerable to cut-price competition from large companies as idealism has prevented lowering of standards and quality;

(*c*) management is hampered by democratic procedures and can be slow to react, for example, to changing fashions and developments;

(*d*) investments pay only a fixed rate of interest (unlike shares) and cannot be bought and sold;

(*e*) the co-operative ideal suffers with increasing prosperity and seems to have been most successful in poor times.

19. Types of co-operative ownership. There is a variety of co-operative organization, including *housing co-operatives,* (formed by people who buy or rent housing and manage and maintain them collectively), and *farmers' co-operatives* for obtaining supplies at reasonable prices.

(*a*) *Co-operative societies.* The well-known logo of the Co-op is visible in every main shopping centre in Britain as one of the main retailing chains. Most shops are separately owned by local co-operative societies but many are now owned by Co-operative Retail Services which has become the largest society. Until recently the Co-op was the largest retailer of groceries in Britain but its market share has fallen steadily in the face of competition from other large retail chains.

(*b*) *The Co-operative Wholesale Society.* The CWS is the central federal organization of the consumer co-operatives and is owned by the independent retail societies.

20. Co-operative ownership today. In the world recession of the 1970s, co-operative ownership was viewed as a potential route for business and industrial survival. In countries such as Italy it has widely developed into fields such as banking, and Spain has its successful Montdragon co-operatives.

In Britain, the 1970s saw a revival of co-operative organization as part of the the attempt to rescue ailing firms by government initiative and funds. Two of the most important developments were:

(*a*) the Co-operative Ownership Act 1976 which provided funds to the Industrial Common Ownership Movement (ICOM) for support to co-operatives; and

(*b*) the Co-operative Development Agency Act 1978 which set up the Co-operative Development Agency (CDA) to promote and represent the interests of co-operative principles.

Many co-operatives provided with aid in the 1970s failed, such as the Scottish Daily News. The number of co-operatives in existence in Britain continues to increase, however, from 300 in 1980 to 1500 in 1986. They are generally in small-scale, craft-based activities organized on a neighbourhood basis, often with part-time labour. There has been some development of co-operative ownership in developing fields of business such as computer software where no tradition of business organization exists, and also in businesses traditionally dominated by partnerships such as architecture. In a sense, co-operatives cannot be judged simply in business terms, and as developments continue to be made they could emerge as a strong form of business organization.

The public sector

21. Definition. The public sector has been traditionally dominated by large public enterprises, many of which have now been privatized, i.e. have become part of the private sector by the sale of shares to the public. In addition to these nationalized industries, the public sector includes the productive activities of central government departments and local authorities. Government departments and local authorities supply social needs such as medical care, road building and maintenance, and education and training facilities, while public corporations play an important role in the transport and energy industries. Finance for the public sector is largely raised by the government, and the objective is to supply the public with essential services, although within an increasingly tighter financial framework. Although disagreement is always present about the extent of government involvement in business and industry, most countries have some element of public enterprise, for example, the state-owned firm of Renault in France and the high level of government ownership of Volkswagen in the Federal Republic of Germany.

22. Government involvement. There are a number of reasons for the existence of government involvement in business and industrial activities.

(*a*) To avoid waste by duplication of services. This explains the reason for state ownership in many countries of public utilities such as water supply;

(*b*) Some industries, such as coal and steel can be operated more efficiently as monopolies because the nature of the industry means that only one producer may be able to obtain economies of scale;

(*c*) A service may be regarded as vital to a country as a whole, e.g. broadcasting;

(*d*) It may be important for a country to ensure the effective development of a new industry, e.g. nuclear power;

(*e*) An industry's development may suffer by not attracting sufficient capital from private sources and government support may be essential.

The public corporation

23. Definition. A public corporation is an organization created by Act of Parliament which is owned by the public. The public corporation has been accepted in Britain as the most effective form of organization for running the nationalized industries in a commercial way whilst maintaining a strong element of supervision by the state. Since the Post Office became the first state-owned service in the 17th century, a number of activities were taken into the public sector, including the BBC (British Broadcasting Corporation), and Bank of England, and parts of the transport and energy industries. Many nationalized industries, such as gas and telecommunications have now been sold back to the private sector.

24. Organization. A public corporation is brought into being by Act of Parliament and becomes the responsibility of a Minister in the government who will provide 'general directives' regarding its operation. The Minister will then appoint a Board, headed by a Chairman, to be responsible for the day-to-day running of the enterprise. Parliamentary supervision of the industries takes the form of examination of annual reports submitted to it by the board, and the affairs of nationalized industries are investigated by parliamentary committees such as the Select Committee on Nationalized Industries and the Public Accounts Committee. External supervision of nationalized industries is carried out by the Monopolies and Mergers Commission. Each public corporation has the statutory duty to establish a consumer council to represent the interests of consumers, for example, the Post Office Users' National Council.

25. Finance. The financial obligations of each public corporation are stated in the statute by which it was set up, and although the financial framework within which it operates is set by the government, its finances are separate from it. The government controls the amount of finance nationalized industries can raise from external sources by imposing *external financing limits*, and establishes a *required rate of return* to ensure investment is used effectively. *Financial targets* are also set by the government to provide a means of measuring operating efficiency in industries in which they have monopoly powers.

The finance of nationalized industries has always given rise to disagreement over the extent to which they are expected to provide a service to the nation or to behave as commercial enterprises. The original obligation of most of the industries was simply to 'break-even', but other considerations have subsequently been introduced to seek greater efficiency. Encouragement is now provided by the government for the nationalised industries to act as commercial enterprises as far as possible, and more finance for investment is now being raised from internally generated funds.

26. Criticism of nationalized industries.

(*a*) they are costly because of the lack of competition.

(*b*) they are inefficient because a bureaucratic style of organization is unsuitable for the management of a commercial enterprise.

(*c*) they result in reduction of choice for consumers.

(*d*) competitors claim they are discriminated against, for example the government may give a public corporation preferential treatment.

It is difficult to judge the importance of these criticisms as the expectations of the nationalized industries are a matter of political debate. To some extent it is inevitable that they should be expected to provide a service for the national good, such as a comprehensive rail service to all parts of the land, but it is difficult to decide upon an acceptable cost to the state for this. The various criticisms put forward have led to the privatization of many of the nationalized industries since 1979.

Central government

27. **Introduction.** A number of services are provided directly by government departments, and many aspects of business in the private sector are regulated and controlled by central government through the various departments and agencies. Defence and law and order have long been government responsibilities, but many other aspects of state involvement in business have developed in more recent times, for example, regulation of business practices and the provision of job training facilities. Each department is staffed by civil servants who are responsible to the minister in charge of that department.

28. **Government departments.** Some of the most important government departments are the following.

(*a*) The *Treasury* is responsible for overall financial and economic policy. Government policy has four main objectives:

(*i*) to maintain a balance of payments with other trading nations,

(*ii*) to guard against inflation,

(*iii*) to seek full employment, and

(*iv*) to stimulate economic growth.

The Treasury co-ordinates the policies of various government departments and implements the government's policies by bringing about changes in interest rates and the money supply, and by adjustments in levels of taxation and public spending.

(*b*) The *Department of Trade and Industry* is responsible for relations between the government and industry. It oversees several nationalized industries, promotes exports, and provides a regulatory framework for competition and company policy. It provides various schemes of financial aid to industry, for example, for regional development.

(*c*) The *Department of Employment* is responsible for the general task of ensuring that the labour force is adequate to the demands of business and industry. In recent years it has sponsored a number of schemes to improve the skills of the labour force by job training programmes and facilities, often in conjunction with agencies such as the Training Commission and Industrial Training Boards. It also provides advice and guidance in the small business sector of the economy, in conjunction with bodies such as the Scottish and Welsh Development Agencies.

(*d*) The *Department of Education and Science*, in addition to its responsibilities for all phases of education has, in recent years participated in the work of vocational training.

(*e*) The *Department of the Environment* has a number of functions, including overseeing of the nationalized transport industries, responsibility for local government, and general aspects of the environment such as pollution control.

29. Government agencies. In addition to government departments, there are a number of agencies which are responsible for various business activities and functions.

(*a*) The Training Commission has the general responsibility for evaluating the labour needs of the country and of providing for training by such schemes as the Job Training Scheme.

(*b*) The British Technology Group exists to promote new technology by funding research and assisting in the commercial applications of that research.

(*c*) The British Overseas Trade Board helps exporters in selling in overseas markets.

Local Government

30. Responsibilities and operation. Local authorities are responsible for carrying out many services such as education and public health on behalf of central government, and for providing many locally-based services such as refuse collection. Services are usually administered by committees of the council and by departments such as Highways, Education, and Health within the authority. Services are financed by locally raised rates and by grants from central government. Unlike some other countries, local authorities in Britain cannot engage in business activities without statutory approval, and thus there has not been the possibility of the sort of municipal enterprise seen elsewhere. Local authorities have therefore generally to be content to provide civic amenities such as leisure centres and theatres, but in recent years have participated in initiatives such as setting up local enterprise agencies (*see* 2:25).

Case 4 Marks & Spencer Plc

Marks & Spencer Plc is Britain's biggest retailer with an annual turnover in excess of £4 billion, and sells only one brand – St. Michael – to its 14 million customers each week.

The origins of the firm go back to 1884 when Michael Marks set up a stall, as a sole proprietor, in Leeds Market selling haberdashery – every item priced at only one penny! By 1894 Marks, by then with a chain of eight stalls, needed money for expansion, and formed a partnership with Tom Spencer – the birth of Marks & Spencer. In 1903 continuing growth of the partnership into more market stalls and shops prompted the partners to turn their business into a limited company. Control was divided equally between the partners but the Articles of Association did not provide for the role of their successors. The sons of the original partners inherited their interests, but by 1917 Simon Marks had control of the business and became its chairman, a post he held until the 1960s.

After the second world war, the company developed its interests in quality control of the products it sold by setting up close links with their suppliers. Growth continued so that in 1926, with 125 stores throughout Britain, Marks & Spencer became a public limited company (plc). The firm has always been conscious of its family atmosphere, however, a number of the directors and top managers having spent all their working lives with the firm, and control has remained in the hands of the Marks family.

Growth of the firm has continued in recent years with a number of new initiatives taken. New product lines have ben introduced, such as foodstuffs in the 1960s, home furnishing in the 1970s, and furniture in 1987, and its own chargecard is produced by its subsidiary firm, Marks & Spencer Financial Services. It has become Britain's biggest clothing exporter, and established a number of overseas stores in Europe, some of them as franchises. Over 200 stores have been acquired in Canada, operating as subsidiary companies with separate identities, and one of the companies – D'Allairds, specialising in ladies fashions – is opening stores in the USA. The worldwide expansion of M & S now seems a far cry from the original stall in Leeds market.

Progress test 4

1. Distinquish between the private and public sectors. (**1**)
2. List the forms of organization in the private sector. (**2**)
3. Note the advantages and disadvantages of the sole proprietor. (**3**)
4. Describe the main features of a Partnership. (**4**)
5. What do you understand by 'incorporation'? (**6**)
6. How is a company (*a*) formed, and (*b*) dissolved? (**8,9**)
7. Discuss the advantages and disadvantages of companies. (**10**)
8. What is franchising? Explain how it works. (**11,12**)
9. What are the advantages and disadvantages of franchising? (**13,14**)
10. What is co-operative ownership and how did it develop? (**16,17**)
11. How important are co-operatives today? (**20**)
12. What is a public corporation? (**23**)
13. Why are some industries nationalized? (**22**)
14. What criticisms can be made of nationalized industries? (**26**)
15. Note briefly the role of government departments in business. (**28**)
16. What are the main responsibilities of local authorities? (**30**)

5

Business finance

Finance

1. Definition. Finance can be described as the function of obtaining and using funds for business, as and when needed, in both the private and public sectors. In a modern economy the role of financial management is vital, as it is involved in most business activities – the purchase of raw materials, hiring of equipment, promotion of a new product, and remuneration of staff. In every business, the careful consideration of the way in which funds are raised, and the monitoring of the way they are used, is a vital aspect of the firm's operation.

Capital

2. Definition. Capital, in its simplest sense, can be defined as money. But in the business sense it has to be in a form in which it can become productive, i.e. as the plant and machinery, equipment, and raw materials necessary to produce goods and services. The health of a business can be seen from its *balance sheet* (*see* Fig. 5.1), and the capital of a business can be seen as the amount by which business assets exceed liabilities.

3. Types of capital. Several forms of capital can be distinquished:

(*a*) *fixed capital*, which includes items such as the land, buildings, and vehicles which are more or less a permanent feature

Liabilities		Assets	
Capital		Fixed assets	
Preference shares		Premises	
Ordinary shares		Equipment	
Reserves		Vehicles	
Debentures		Current assets	
Current liabilities		Stock	
	£	Debtors	
		Cash at bank	
		Cash in hand	
			£

Figure 5.1 *Balance sheet of a limited company*

of the business. These are often referred to as the 'fixtures and fittings';

(*b*) *circulating capital*, or 'working capital' which is normally consumed in the production process, such as cash and stock held. A good margin of working capital is usually an indication of the good health of the business;

(*c*) *liquid capital*, e.g. bank balances, which can easily be changed into cash;

(*d*) *social capital*, which is in the form of schools, hospitals, libraries, and other resources available for general public use.

Sources of finance

4. Introduction. There are two major sources of funds for business – *debt capital* which is finance obtained through borrowing, and *equity capital*, obtained by owners' increased investment or by the sale of part of their interests in the firm. Sources of finance may be examined as those mainly for short-term finance, and those for long-term finance.

5. Short-term finance. Finance which is available over a period of up to three years is regarded as short-term. Such finance may be necessary to cover normal fluctuations in a firm's trading position or possibly seasonal variations.

(*a*) *Savings*. Many small businesses are set up on the basis of the accumulated savings of their owners. Similarly, expansion of the business is often achieved by profits 'ploughed back' by owners into the firm.

(*b*) *Private loans*. A loan to establish a business can often be more cheaply secured from a friend or relative of the owner.

(*c*) *Banks*. Although banks in Britain have traditionally preferred to lend to private customers for consumer purchases, there has been in recent years an increasing trend towards providing funds for business. Bank lending is usually of two types: *overdraft*, if the amount or term required is not precisely known: or by the more usual means of a *loan* when a certain sum is needed for a specific purpose. A higher rate of interest may be charged on a bank loan, and the bank may require security.

(*d*) *Finance houses*. Small businesses may borrow from finance houses by means of hire purchase. A deposit, typically for an item of equipment, may be paid to the supplier to whom the finance house then pays the remainder of the purchase price. The borrower pays off the hire purchase debt to the finance house over an agreed period of time at a specific rate of interest.

(*e*) *Leasing*. Leasing has become an increasingly popular means of obtaining vehicles, office fittings, and other types of equipment. It has the advantage of avoiding laying out cash for outright purchase.

(*f*) *Trade credit*. In the normal course of business, a firm is likely to owe suppliers for goods received. A period of time between receipt of the goods and payment for them can be seen as a useful form of short-term finance, although it would involve the loss of any discount offered for prompt payment.

(*g*) *Debt factoring*. Another means of short-term credit on a continuing basis, especially in international trade, is by selling debts to a factoring house which then settles them as they arise.

6. Long-term finance. Finance which may be needed for up to ten years is termed long-term finance. The need may be for the construction of new buildings, the replacement of plant, or for the purchase of fixed assets with a long life. Although wider share ownership is being encouraged in Britain, most of the capital for business is provided by institutional investors such as pension funds, insurance companies, investment trusts, and unit trusts.

(*a*) *Banks*. Commercial banks are willing to make long-term loans for business, for example, for plant and machinery, and especially to small firms. The more usual source of long-term bank lending is, however, the merchant banks who normally arrange large-scale loans.

(*b*) *Insurance companies*. Insurance companies take in premiums from policyholders for a wide variety of risks, and pay out in compensation for losses sustained. Many policies taken out are on a long-term basis, for example, life assurance, endowments, and annuities, and premiums can be invested to provide part of the cost of meeting claims. Insurance companies invest widely, and are an important source of capital for companies.

(*c*) *Pension funds*. Pension funds such as those of British Coal and the Post Office, have become a major sector of the financial market and are a source of capital for business. These private pension funds are 'funded' i.e. the contributions paid by members are invested in assets, the returns on which pay for the pensions. As shares in companies are the most important assets held by pension funds they represent an important source of finance for business.

(*d*) *Specialist organizations*. Capital can be obtained from certain specialist organizations. Investors in Industry plc, for example, provide funds to small and large companies for periods of up to twenty years

7. Securities. The problems involved in obtaining finance for the small business may prompt owners to set up the business as a company, in order that capital may be obtained by issuing stocks and shares for sale. A share is, as the name suggests, ownership of a part of an enterprise obtained by payment, and thus represents a means whereby the owners can increase their capital by making shares in the business available to other people. While individual share ownership is growing, investment trusts and unit trusts are

Finance needed in ...	Short Term	... Or	Long Term
For ...	e.g. General working capital, some plant and machinery		e.g. New building, expansion of the firm
Mainly supplied by ...	Savings Private loans Clearing banks Finance houses Leasing companies Factoring companies		Clearing banks Merchant banks Insurance companies Pension funds Investors in industry Public sector agencies Securities

Figure 5.2 *Sources of finance for business*

popular for small investments as the managers of the trusts spread their assets over a number of investments and thus reduce the risks.

There are two types of company – the private company and the public, or joint-stock company. A private company (*see* **4:10**) cannot make shares available to the general public, while the far more common form – the public company – is allowed to make an unlimited issue of shares. In Britain the buying and selling of shares traditionally takes place on the Stock Exchange (*see* **12**).

8. Types of share. The main types of shares are:

(*a*) *Ordinary shares* (also called *equities*). Profits made by the company are paid out to shareholders – after all other claims have been met – in the form of dividends. For the shareholder, ordinary shares represent a risk, as the investment may not earn anything if the company has a poor trading year. On the other hand shares in a company which is prospering would obviously continue to increase in value. Ordinary shares also offer the advantage that the holders carry full voting rights in the company.

(*b*) Preference shares. Holders have priority over ordinary shareholders in respect of dividends, and also prior claim upon the capital of the company in the event of liquidation. Preference shares do not carry voting rights and may be cumulative, in which case dividends unpaid in one year may be paid in a subsequent year before ordinary shareholders receive their dividends.

(*c*) Debentures. Debentures are often referred to as loan stock as they are loans to the company rather than shares. They carry a very low risk as they earn a fixed rate of interest which the company is legally liable to pay.

Shares in companies which are highly regarded as being both safe and offering good returns are known as *blue chips*, while stocks issued by the government – rather than a company – are referred to as *gilt-edged* or *gilts*.

9. Share dealing. Companies wishing to raise capital do so by issuing shares and debentures through issuing houses and underwriters. Collectively, this is known as the new issue market, but it is always necessary to have a secondary market on which securities can be bought and sold. In Britain this function is served by the Stock Exchange which is one of the largest markets in the world, and wider share ownership has been encouraged by access to stockbroking services operated by banks and by developments such as Debenham's Share Centres within retail stores.

The Stock Exchange

10. Definition. The Stock Exchange (now The International Stock Exchange of the United Kingdom and the Republic of Ireland Limited) provides a primary market for raising capital for private industry and the government, and a secondary market for the buying and selling of existing shares. Its motto is 'My word is my bond' and it is proud of its reputation for fair dealing.

11. Organization. The Stock Exchange is an independent organization, registered as a Recognised Investment Exchange (RIE) under the Financial Services Act 1987.

(*a*) *Self-regulation.* The Act was intended to establish a structure of self-regulation within a statutory framework, and the Stock

Exchange became a self-regulating organization (SRO) responsible for the conduct of business between its members and clients. All SROs, including the Stock Exchange, are overseen by one central agency – the Securities and Investment Board (SIB) – whose rules set the standards which SROs must apply in their supervision of their own members. The Council of the Stock Exchange, elected by members, is the governing body which sets rules and enforces standards.

(*b*) *Membership*. Stock Exchange member firms have to undergo rigorous admission procedures. Since the *Big Bang* of 1986 all member firms have 'single capacity' to buy and sell shares for their clients, (unlike the previous separation of the role of broker and jobber). Now all members combine the role of broker/dealer, although some are called *market makers* as they are prepared to buy or sell shares at all times, that is, 'making a market' in them.

12. Operation. Raising finance for business by 'going public', that is, by selling shares to the public, can be an effective means of raising capital without incurring interest charges or by having to lose control in a business. There are a number of stages involved in a company flotation:

(*a*) The company has to obtain advice, usually from a merchant bank, and obtain the services of a stockbroker to sponsor it.

(*b*) The Stock Exchange will examine the company's trading history, profit and loss account, management record, and prospects.

(*c*) The number and type of shares to be issued has to be decided, and, if possible, *underwritten*, that is, bought when available, by banks or institutions such as pension funds or insurance companies.

(*d*) The company's *Prospectus* will be issued, giving details of the company and details and price of the shares it is offering for sale.

(*e*) Applications for shares are made by the public, and allocated.

(*f*) Finally, on 'flotation day' shares are traded on the Stock Exchange, and the success of the company's launch measured by how many of the shares will have been bought and by how much they rise in price.

Before a company's shares can be traded on the Stock Exchange it has to become 'listed', that is, its financial affairs have to be approved by the Council (the controlling body). For many years there was only one market (the listed market for well-established companies) on the floor of the Stock Exchange. In 1980, however, a second market was created within the Stock Exchange – the Unlisted Securities Market (USM) intended to cater for the capital needs of companies unable to meet the requirements for 'full listing' on the Exchange (*see* Case 5). In 1987 a further development in this direction saw the establishment of the *Third Market* for shares in companies which are very young and have good growth prospects.

13. Recent development. Considerable changes in the operation of the Stock Exchange took place at the time of the Big Bang in October 1986. The most important results of the changes were:

(*a*) members of the Stock Exchange can negotiate commissions with their clients whereas previously commissions were fixed by the Exchange;

(*b*) all member firms have 'single capacity' to buy and sell shares for their clients, (unlike the previous separation of the role of broker and jobber);

(*c*) wider membership is now possible by allowing outside firms to own member firms of the Exchange, whilst previously control had to be in the hands of individual members.

One of the most dramatic changes was the introduction of the electronic market by which the traditional form of trading which took place on the floor of the Exchange has been almost entirely replaced by SEAQ (Stock Exchange Automated Quotations). Prices are quoted on SEAQ by the Exchange's own viewdata network *TOPIC* and trading then takes place by telephone.

14. Co-ops. Co-operative societies are organized under the Industrial and Provident Societies Act, 1965 and their issue of shares differs from that of public companies. Fixed interest is paid on shares held by their customers, who receive profits in the form of dividends. Shares can only be bought and sold from the society and are not available on the open market.

Finance in the public sector

15. Introduction. The public sector in the UK consists of central government, local authorities, and public corporations. All are important providers of goods and services and have to raise money in various ways to meet their costs. The public sector has grown considerably over the years since the last century when the government's only commitments were defence and law and order. The public sector is a vital part of the economy, employing about 25 per cent of the working population and taking 25 per cent of total investment. In recent years public sector organizations have been encouraged to adopt a more commercial approach to their operations, for example, some health service functions and services such as refuse disposal have been sub-contracted to private operators.

16. Public goods and services. These are goods and services which are provided collectively for the benefit of all, and which, it is assumed, would not be provided satisfactorily in a free market economy. Public goods and services are non-exclusive in that they benefit everyone, for example, defence and health-care, and all have to contribute to their provision by taxation which the state is able to impose with the force of law.

17. Financing central government. Central government undertakes a large part of public expenditure directly, through departments of state for whom a minister is responsible to Parliament. The most important services provided are social security, defence, and education (*see* 2:**17**). In addition, central government provides grants to local authorities and to public corporations.

Most of the finance to provide services is raised by taxation (see later). A large proportion of public spending is also paid for by borrowing, and the total amount which the government needs to finance its services and also those of the public corporations and local authorities is called the public sector borrowing requirement (PSBR). The PSBR is financed mainly from the sale of gilt-edged stock and national savings, as well as by borrowing from banks and from overseas. The PSBR has been reduced in recent years with the privatization of some of the nationalized industries.

18. Local authorities. Councils at county, borough, district, and community levels provide a range of services. In many cases these may be the purely local services of refuse collection or maintenance of public amenities, but also include at county level the provision of services such as education, environmental services, and personal social services. Local government is financed from the following sources:

(*a*) Rates are levied upon the value of property by district councils, and are calculated at a specific rate in the pound. Certain types of property, such as agricultural land and buildings, are exempt from rates, and rebates can be claimed by householders whose income may be below a certain figure. The rating system provides an independent source of finance for local authorities but it has progressively become a smaller proportion of their total income and it is to be replaced.

The Green Paper *Paying for Local Government* (Cmnd 9714) published in Janauary, 1986 proposed that domestic rates should be phased out over a period of ten years and be replaced by a flat rate *community charge*, payable by everyone over the age of eighteen. The proposals are based on the need to ensure local accountability for the services provided. The new system is to be introduced in Scotland in 1989 and is expected to be introduced in England and Wales in 1990.

(*b*) Approximately half of local authority spending is financed by grants from central government. Most of the finance is contained within the *rate support grant* (RSG) but specific grants are also paid for certain services such as education. The rate support grant consists of two elements – a block grant which is intended to allow councils to provide a comparable standard of service, and a domestic rate relief grant to reimburse councils for the cost of giving rate relief.

(*c*) Councils also borrow from central government via the Public Works Loan Board. They can also borrow from the money market and issue bonds for sale to the public but the government has controlled raising finance in this way in recent years.

(*d*) Income is received for many of the services provided by local authorities, for example, rents for housing and charges for use of car parks and leisure facilities.

19. Public corporations. Public corporations provide a number of essential services in the transport and energy sectors of the economy, and enjoy a measure of financial independence within the public sector.

Attempts have been made to treat the financial arrangements of the nationalized industries as far as possible as commercial organizations. Targets are set for returns on investment, and public corporations who need finance have to obtain it from the central government by the National Loans Fund (NLF) while those who achieve a surplus pay it into that fund. Much of their expenditure is, of course, financed by their undistributed profits, and they can also borrow from banks. The government imposes external financing limits (EFLs) upon the nationalized industries to control the amount of finance the industries can borrow.

Taxation

20. Definition. Taxation is the means by which governments obtain funds from individuals, organizations, and property, to finance the provision of services.

21. Principles of taxation. There are a number of important principles upon which tax systems should be based, some of them originally established by Adam Smith in The Wealth of Nations in 1776:

(*a*) *Simplicity.* If people are required to pay taxes they should be easily understood.

(*b*) *Certainty.* Taxpayers should be aware of what the basis of taxation is, or what items are liable to tax.

(*c*) *Convenience.* Tax collection should be, as far as possible, in a form which is convenient for the taxpayer, for example, PAYE (pay as you earn) is a system whereby tax payments are deducted immediately from earnings and avoids the possibility of large tax bills building up.

(*d*) *Economy*. A tax should be economical to collect: the cost of collecting taxes on income in Britain is a small proportion of the income obtained from it, while the cost of collecting taxes on capital is higher.

(*e*) *Equity*. The burden of taxation should be evenly spread so that all citizens of a country contribute fairly. In most countries a system of progressive taxation ensures that in general those on higher incomes pay a higher proportion in taxation than the poor. Regressive taxation takes a larger proportion of lower incomes – the tax on an item consumed by a wide section of the community is a larger proportion of a low income.

22. Functions of taxation. Initially, taxes were raised in order to finance government expenditure, but other purposes are also served:

(*a*) *Raising revenue*. The primary aim of taxation is still to meet the needs of government over a wide area of public expenditure.

(*b*) *Economic policy*. Taxation is now used as part of governmental control of the economy, for example, by combating inflation or encouraging employment.

(*c*) *Redistribution of national income*. Taxation helps to lessen the inequalities of income by redistributing income from the rich to the poor, for example, by progressive taxation whereby increasing earnings are taxed more heavily.

The British tax system

23. Introduction. Parliament has to authorize the levying of taxes by passing an annual Finance Act. This usually follows the Budget in which changes in taxation have been proposed. The Chancellor of the Exchequer is also empowered to raise taxes by use of the *regulator* by which the rates of commodity taxes can be changed.

The administration of taxation is the responsibility of two government departments. The Board of Inland Revenue collects taxes on income and capital, and national insurance contributions. Most of its revenue is paid by the PAYE system (*see* **21**) by which the tax on income is deducted at source, that is, before it is actually paid as earnings. The Board of Customs and Excise is responsible for taxes on expenditure such as import duties and VAT (value added tax).

In addition to these two departments, motor vehicle licence duties are collected by the Department of Transport, while local rates are collected by local authorities.

Taxes can be broadly divided into those which are *direct*, (i.e. on the income and capital of people and organizations), and *indirect*, (i.e. those which are collected as taxes from the sales of commodities).

24. Direct taxes.

(*a*) *Personal taxation.* Income tax is collected by the PAYE system and provides the biggest yield of any single tax. It is a progressive tax, paid at higher rates of tax as income increases (see Fig. 2.1). These rates of tax apply to both earned income, that is, most forms of wages or salaries, and to unearned or investment income. Income tax is levied on gross income, with various allowances granted which mean that a certain level of income is free of tax. Everyone has a personal allowance, and additional allowances may be made, for example, for mortgage payments, life assurance premiums, and superannuation contributions.

(*b*) *Company taxation.* Companies pay corporation tax on their profits, after deduction of certain allowances for interest on loans and depreciation of plant and machinery. The main rate of corporation tax is 35 per cent, with a reduced rate of 25 per cent for small companies with profits of less than £100,000 a year.

(*c*) *Capital taxes.* The two main forms of taxation on capital are:

(*i*) *Capital gains tax*, paid on the sale of assets. There are two rates—25 per cent and 40 per cent but exemption is granted on gains up to £5,000 in any one year. Certain assets, such as a person's main residence and car are normally exempt;

(*ii*) *Inheritance tax*, which is paid on transfers of personal wealth made up to seven years before the death of the donor. The first £110,000 is exempt from tax but rates of tax are progressively higher on transfers above that level.

(*d*) *Petroleum revenue tax.* This tax (currently 75 per cent) is charged to licensees of oilfields in the UK and on the Continental Shelf, on the profits from the production of oil and gas. Allowances are paid for costs incurred in exploration and development.

25. Indirect taxes.

(*a*) *Value added tax* (VAT). VAT is charged at each stage in the production and distribution of goods and services. It is currently paid at a rate of 15 per cent. It is a broadly based tax paid on most goods and services, but relief may be obtained either by:

(*i*) zero-rating (e.g. on foods, books, and fuels),whereby the supplier does not charge the customer any tax and is able to reclaim tax paid by him to his suppliers; or by

(*ii*) exemption, by which customers are not charged VAT but the supplier cannot reclaim any he would have paid himself. Exemption is granted in a wide range of activities such as land, insurance, and postal services.

(*b*) *Customs duties*. Customs duties are payable on goods imported, in accordance with EC regulations.

(*c*) *Excise duties*. Excise duties are imposed on home-produced products such as alcohol and cigarettes. Excise duties are also paid on betting and on car licensing.

26. Other forms of taxation. In addition to the main forms of taxation above, National Insurance contributions are paid towards the cost of the National Insurance Fund and the National Health Service. Local authority rates are one of the main forms of income for local government.

Case 5 The Unlisted Securities Market

The Stock Exchange has traditionally been the source of capital for established companies. During the 1970s, however, the number of firms being listed at the Stock Exchange was falling as small businesses found strict Stock Exchange regulations and the high cost of listing difficult to meet. In 1980, therefore, a new market was opened – the Unlisted Securities Market (USM) – to serve the needs of smaller and less mature companies. The aim was to provide a market where small and medium size firms could obtain finance without loss of control by having their shares publicly traded.

In order to encourage newer, small-scale businesses, the USM's requirements are less strict than those required for a full listing, e.g. companies which have been trading for only three years can enter the USM whereas a five year trading record is needed for a full listing. Accounting requirements are also less demanding – in place of the formal accounts needed for full listing the USM accepts a set of financial statistics. And an important attraction is that the USM requires that companies need only make 10 per cent of their shares available to the public – instead of the 25 per cent demanded for a full listing – which naturally allows smaller firms to retain their independence. This has also provided an opportunity for employees to share in the success of a new and developing business. A simplified procedure for entry to the USM requires firms to have a sponsor, accept the USM general undertaking, and place a box advert in a national daily paper to announce the flotation to the public.

The USM was an immediate success – trading started in only eleven companies but by 1988 there were over 600. Among the firms which have been able to expand by raising capital on the USM have been developing enterprises such as Pineapple, Tie Rack, and Sock Shop. A feature of the market has been its attraction for female entrepreneurs – Anita Roddick of the Body Shop and Sophie Mirman of Sock Shop – and American firms such as Mrs Field's, the cookie store chain.

Many firms have progressed from the USM to full listing on the Stock Exchange, and the success of the USM encouraged the Stock Exchange to set up The Third Market in 1987 – to encourage even younger businesses with growth prospects.

Progress test 5

1. What is finance? (**1**)
2. Define capital. How many types are there? (**2,3**)
3. What are the main sources of short-term finance? (**5**)
4. What are the main sources of long-term finance? (**6**)
5. What are securities? (**7**)
6. Distinquish between ordinary shares and reference shares (**8**)
7. What is the Stock Exchange? Describe its membership and role. (**10**)

8. Explain the nature of 'self-regulation' at the Stock Exchange. (**11**)
9. Describe how shares are traded on the Stock Exchange. (**12**)
10. What changes have recently taken place at the Stock Exchange? (**13**)
11. How are co-operatives financed? (**14**)
12. How do local authorities finance their services? (**18**)
13. Explain how public corporations raise finance. (**19**)
14. Define taxation. (**20**)
15. What are the principles upon which taxation should be based? (**21**)
16. What are the functions of taxation? (**22**)
17. What are the main direct taxes in Britain? (**24**)
18. What are the main indirect taxes? (**25**)
19. What advantages does the USM offer a developing business? (**Case 5**)

6

Internal organization and communications

Organization

1. Definition. Organization is the process whereby a structure is created in which resources can be used effectively to achieve overall objectives. In order for any form of business to be successful, effective organization is essential so that people and resources can be co-ordinated, plans can be carried out and objectives can be achieved. A structure is necessary for responsibilities to be clearly defined and channels of information understood so that interaction can take place between the various divisions and directed towards the general objectives of the business.

2. Organization structure. Organization has to be based upon several important principles.

(*a*) *Objectives* have to be established, graded from the overall objectives of the enterprise to the individual targets of each employee. The main activities of the firm have to be analyzed in order that a structure may be drawn up in which divisions, departments, and other working groups can be allocated clearly-defined functions and responsibilities.

(*b*) Authority and responsibility must be allocated.

(*i*) *Responsibility* can be defined as the obligation to perform certain functions, and each division of an enterprise has to be certain of the nature and extent of its responsibilities.

(*ii*) *Authority* is the power to make decisions and to act upon them. When authority is spread widely throughout an organization it is said to be *decentralised*, whilst a *centralised* system occurs when authority is held by a few centrally placed managers.

(*iii*) *Delegation* is the act of allocating certain activities to other people. Although authority for various functions can be delegated, the ultimate responsibility for those functions remains with the person who delegated them.

(*iv*) *Accountability* can be defined as being the liability of people with authority for carrying out activities for which they are responsible.

(*c*) *Coordination* between the various divisions of the enterprise has to be effected in order that work is directed towards the achievement of the overall aims of the firm.

(*d*) *Communications* are vital in ensuring that all parts of an organization are aware of activities relevant to them. Communication becomes of greater importance as a firm grows in size, and poor communication is frequently the cause of problems within an organization.

(*e*) *Flexibility* is an important principle in ensuring that the enterprise can respond to changing conditions. There has been a tendency in recent years to develop the complexity of organization for its own sake, especially at a time when the pace of change is quickening.

3. Types of organization. Organizations can be classified according to their internal structure. There are several main types.

(*a*) *Line organization*. This is based upon a direct form of authority from the top to the bottom of the organization. It is the oldest form of organization and typical of a military structure in which people are responsible to one senior person only.

This form of organization has the advantage of being simple and easily understood, with clearly defined areas of authority and responsibility. Discipline is easier to maintain, and decision-making is simplified, as usually only one superior may need to be consulted. A disadvantage is that a manager may have a number of responsibilities and is not effective over all of them, a factor which makes this form of organization less suitable for larger firms. It also tends to be a rather rigid form of organization which is not able to react positively to change.

(*b*) *Functional organization*. This form of organization occurs when authority for certain functions within the firm is assigned to specific people. It was developed to overcome the main disadvantage of line organization in concentrating too many varied responsibilities in one manager.

Functional organization has the advantage of making effective use of experts either as line managers or as advisers to line managers. Coordination and control are both improved upon by having clearly defined responsibilities assigned for specific functions, The main disadvantage of functional organization is that overlapping of functions inevitably occurs, with the result that employees may not know who has authority in some situations.

(*c*) *Line and staff organization*. This is a form of organization in which the direct line of authority present in line organization and the responsibility for specific functions found in functional organization are combined. It usually means that line managers are responsible for decisions while staff managers make recommendations and act in an advisory capacity.

The advantages are those of each type the rapid decision-making of line organization and the expert knowledge of functional organization.

The disadvantage is that confusion may be caused in terms of who has the authority in some situations, either between line and staff managers or between managers and employees.

(*d*) *Committee organization*. In this form of organization, authority and responsibility are held by a group of individuals rather than by specific managers. It is often found in the public sector in central and local government, and also in certain fields of business and industry, such as research and development. There is usually a structure of committees in which a central decision-making body has ultimate control and is advised by sub-committees.

Committee organization has the advantage of involving many people often co-opted on to committees in decision-making, and in ensuring a good cross-section of viewpoints. Planning and coordination are improved by the inclusion of representatives of all activities, and communications are also usually better.

The main drawback tends to be the slowness of operation, inevitable when many people are involved. Decisions, too, are frequently the result of compromise between opposing views.

4. Organization charts. Organization charts can be used to provide a formal model of the lines of authority and allocation of responsibility in a firm. Charts can be useful in enabling staff to see and understand the operation of a firm, the nature of each employee's responsibility, and the relationship between the various parts of the organization. Charts can be helpful in enabling management to coordinate activities more effectively and also assist new employees to understand the organization. There may, however, be a tendency for charts to become oversimplified and inevitably they may become dated and need frequent revision.

There are several different types of organization chart.

(*a*) The traditional type is the *vertical chart*, often drawn in a pyramid shape and showing direct lines of authority from top to bottom.

(*b*) The *horizontal chart* outlines the organization from left to right so that a hierarchical impression is avoided.

(*c*) A *circular* or *doughnut chart* can provide a more flexible representation of the structure, for example, by showing lines of authority from the centre, possibly with different levels of responsibility shown as concentric circles.

5. Formal and informal organization. Formal lines of authority and responsibility can be shown on an organization chart, but every organization also has *informal organization*. This can best be described as being the grouping together of employees who develop their own informal channels of communication and contact. Informal organization develops out of the inter-relationship of people, often at different levels within the company, who may have common interests, for example, in the organization's social activities. Communication arising from these informal contacts about the affairs of the organization proceeds along the 'grapevine', frequently a valuable form of communication.

Functions of the organization

6. Introduction. There are a number of functions within an organization which are of importance in ensuring that the firm is able to achieve its objectives. Each concentrates upon specific aspects of the work of the firm and will depend to a large extent upon the size of the enterprise. The main functions found in most organizations are:

(*a*) production;
(*b*) purchasing;
(*c*) marketing;
(*d*) personnel;
(*e*) finance;
(*f*) research and development.

7. Production. The function of production describes the process whereby various raw materials or components may be formed into an end product in the form of a good or a service. It will involve the planning and control of resources in the most effective way in order to achieve production of the end product. The nature of the productive process will be affected by factors such as the size of the firm and the level of technology, and improvements may be sought by examining the operation by work study.

There are three main types of process:

(*a*) *unit production*, which may be specifically designed for one customer, and will probably require a flexible approach to how it is produced; .

(*b*) *batch production* or the production of a specific quantity of items, possibly to meet an order or simply to build up stocks;

(c) *flow production*, which takes place when products are required in continuous supply.

Most aspects of the production process are subject to inspection and quality control to ensure that components and materials, as well as the finished product, satisfy standards imposed.

8. Purchasing. Ensuring the supply of raw materials and components of the right quality, in the right quantity, and at the right time, is the responsibility of the purchasing department. It is important that liaison should take place between the purchasing department and the production department so that supplies are sufficient for needs without building up unnecessary stocks. Contact also has to be maintained with the finance department so that payment of goods can be checked against deliveries received. Firms often have centralized buying departments so that costs can be reduced wherever possible by bulk buying. Sometimes firms depend upon one main supplier, possibly as a result of obtaining a quotation for a specified quantity on a contract basis. An alternative approach is for supplies to be obtained from a number of sources in order to minimize the risk of disruptions in delivery.

9. Marketing. The marketing function is concerned with satisfying consumer demand for the firm's product by producing it effectively and at a profit. Market research is essential in monitoring consumer tastes, and firms are very conscious of the need to be consumer-orientated in their approach to marketing. Market trends have to be analyzed so that the firm's advertising strategy can be designed for maximum effect. Marketing will also include the function of distribution of the product and the need for public relations and customer relations.

10. Personnel. The personnel department is responsible for the recruitment of an organization's employees, their training needs, and for ensuring that they are employed effectively. Recruitment depends upon contacts maintained with the various sources of employment, and training needs may be met in a variety of ways. The personnel function also involves such aspects as the promotion and discipline of employees, as well as remuneration and contact with trade unions. The many aspects of legislation relating to safety requirements and standards are also the responsibility of the personnel department, together with any welfare and social facilities.

11. Finance. The function of finance involves running all aspects of a firm's financial affairs and providing financial information when required. It is an essential feature of every organization and its importance can be judged from the difficulties experienced by so many organizations whose products may be viable but whose financial arrangements have been badly handled. All aspects of income and expenditure are handled by the accounts department, and the requirements of the Companies Acts have to be met in such respects as the auditing of accounts by outside auditors and preparation of accounts for shareholders. In larger organizations, specialization of the finance function may result in three main divisions.

(*a*) *Financial accounting* refers to the general preparation of the firms's accounts, indicating the firm's profitability, for directors and shareholders. Within this division there may be separate sections for dealing with taxation and internal audit.

(*b*) *Cost accounting* involves control and analysis of all expenditure, including raw materials, maintenance of plant and machinery, and all factors contributing to the price of the final product.

(*c*) *Management accounting* is the examination and analysis of the firm's budgeting and planning.

12. Research and development. The activity by which new designs, products, and operations are developed within a large organization is known as *research and development* (R & D). Such activity is normally found within manufacturing industries and is sometimes carried out by specialist organizations. Research varies considerably and may be generalized in a large firm, or highly specialized applied research may be concentrated upon the product of a smaller firm. Development refers to the innovation of new processes, materials, or products as a result of the research.

Communication.

13. Definition. Communication is the process whereby information is transmitted in a form in which it can be received and understood. Information may take a number of forms: factual information on technical details; requests for information; orders or instructions to be followed, or observations conveying opinions or attitudes.

14. Importance of communication. It is essential that a communication is effectively received so that some form of action can result. An organization is made up of many separate and different parts, and good communication is vital in ensuring that they are effectively coordinated. As the scale of organization grows, the importance of communication increases: management has to convey intentions clearly and likewise has to depend upon information received from all levels and parts of the organization. Many disputes and disruptions to business activity are the result of a breakdown of communications as wrong impressions are conveyed or misunderstandings occur.

Types of communication

15. Methods of communication. There are various ways in which communication may take place within an organization. In addition to formal methods of communication, accepted as being within the organizational structure of the firm, there are also informal kinds. Another form of classification can be made upon the basis of the direction of communication. Many communications travel *downwards* as information or instructions from a managerial level to employees, while communications are also conveyed *upwards*, possibly as feedback or complaints. Lateral or sideways communication takes place when people or divisions at the same level communicate. A distinction is also made between communication which may be *one-way*, such as information or instructions simply delivered to employees without provision for response, or *two-way*, in which response from those receiving information is a part of the process.

16. Formal methods of communication. The main forms of communication within the organization are as follows.

(*a*) *Written*. Most formal contacts exist in written form: internal memoranda; letters; notices on boards; announcements in pay packets; or company magazines or newletters.

(*b*) *Oral*. Communication in the form of face-to-face contact is constantly taking place within an organization. Many firms also use address systems to broadcast announcements to staff. Interviews may also be a means of one-way or two-way communication, ranging from an interview conducted by management to convey instructions, to job appraisal interviews based on an exchange of views.

(*c*) *Meetings*. Meetings have become an important means of both conveying information and of achieving two-way communication.

Large meetings of employees can be a useful means of conveying important information, possibly to the entire workforce, while small meetings can be a forum for interchange of views and opinions.

(*d*) *Committees*. Formally appointed committees are an important part of the structure of an organization, and may have powers delegated to them to make decisions. They are usually representative of the various parts of the organization, as with interdepartmental committees, and as such are valuable in exchanging views and information. Committees are usually either a permanent feature of the structure as *standing committees*, or *ad hoc committees* set up for a specific purpose and then disbanded.

17. Informal methods of communication. There are inevitably a variety of ways in which communication takes place within an organization outside of formal structures. They can be a useful form of exchanging views and opinions upon aspects of the firm's activities which could otherwise not be expressed formally. The 'grapevine' is a useful source of information at all levels within the firm, and may be invaluable in supplementing formal means of communication. The internal telephone system is probably the main form of informal contact and the most used means of two-way communication.

Case 6 The Wedgwood Group

The small pottery factory established in 1759 by Josiah Wedgwood in Stoke-on-Trent has developed today into an international organization occupying a leading position in many of the world's markets. It is now – as the Wedgwood Group – the major manufacturer in the British ceramic tableware industry, producing 30 per cent of the industry's output, while 60 per cent of its production is exported.

The reputation of Wedgwood was established by its founder's determination to ensure skilled craftsmanship in the ancient skills of throwing, modelling, and decorating. Creativity was another important feature of the firm's development, famous artists often being employed to design new products, many of them – such as

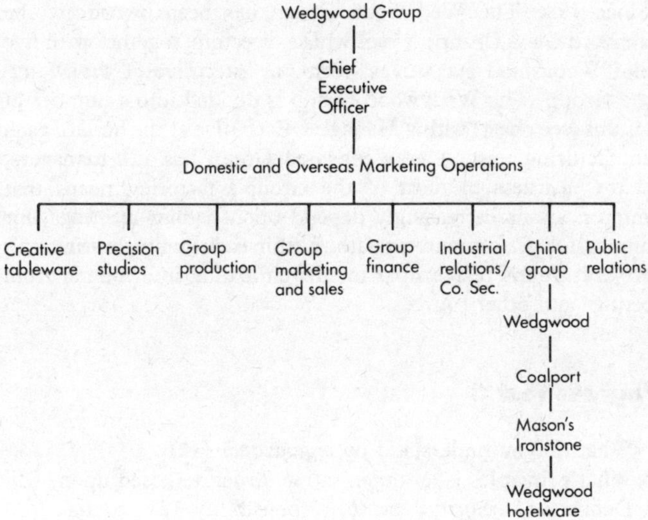

Figure 6.1 *Wedgwood Group—organization*

the Portland Vase, Queen's Ware, and Jasper – gaining international recognition.

In the last twenty years, Wedgwood has expanded rapidly, acquiring many famous and long-established companies, and it is during this period that the Wedgwood Group was formed. From a family firm with 2,000 employees in 1966, it has grown into a public limited company employing over 47,000 people in Britain and overseas. Overseas companies have been set up in USA, Canada, and Japan. Among the firms which are now part of the Wedgwood Group are: Coalport, established in 1750 and one of the most famous of English manufacturers of bone china; Mason's Ironstone which makes decorated earthenware and ornamental ware; J G Meakin, producing fine earthenware tableware; Midwinter, famous for modern designs in tableware; and Johnson Brothers, large-scale manufacturers of tableware. Wedgwood itself has the most extensive and modern factory of its type in the world at Barlaston, combining traditional crafts and the latest technological processes.

Since 1986 The Wedgwood Group has been owned by the Waterford Glass Group, two of whose directors, together with five senior Wedgwood executives, form the executive of the Wedgwood Group. The Wedgwood Group is divided into a number of divisions (see chart) with a Managing Executive at the head of each manufacturing unit. The Wedgwood Group has 120 managers, and the nearness of most of the Group's factories means that communications increasingly depend upon regular meetings, for example, for performance update. Within each manufacturing unit there are groups responsible for disseminating information from meetings and other sources.

Progress test 6

1. What do you understand by *organization*? (**1**)
2. What principles is an organisation structure based upon? (**2**)
3. Define (*a*) authority, and (*b*) responsibility. (**2**)
4. What are the main types of organization? (**3**)
5. Compare the advantages and disadvantages of each one. (**3**)
6. What are organization charts? What are the main types? (**4**)
7. Distinquish between formal and informal organization. (**5**)
8. Describe the main functions of a business organization. (**6-11**)
9. Define communication. (**12**)
10. Why is good communication within an organization important? (**13**)
11. Distinguish between one-way and two-way communication. (**14**)
12. What are the main types of formal communication in a firm? (**15**)
13. What do you understand by *informal communication?* (**16**)
14. Describe how a firm's main functions are represented in the organization of the Wedgwood Group. (**Case 6**)
15. What advantage does the Wedgwood Group have in terms of good communications? (**Case 6**)

Part three

Business services

7

Marketing

Introduction

1. Definition. Marketing is the performance of business activities involved in transfering ownership of goods and services from producer to consumer. The term includes a wide range of activities, such as market research, design, packaging, pricing, selling, distribution, promotion, and advertising – often referred to as the *marketing mix*.

2. The market. The situation in which these business activities linking producer and consumer take place is known as the market. Consumers exert a demand for a particular product, and producers supply the product in return for a money payment. A market need not exist in a physical sense as, for example in the form of a shop, but may describe trading relations between countries, international negotiations over currency or primary commodities, or the increasing use of computerisation, for example, for share-dealing.

3. Market segmentation. In marketing terms, the expression 'the market' is usually used to describe the number of potential purchasers for a particular product. A particular product will not usually be demanded by everyone and it is possible to distinquish sectors of the population likely to be purchasers. The process whereby the total market is divided up and sectors with particular characteristics distinguished is known as *market segmentation*. Some of the more important criteria used in classifying market sectors of the population are:

(*a*) *age*, which is an important determining factor, for instance, young people effect a demand for clothing and leisure facilities while people in a middle-age bracket will spend a large proportion of income upon household goods;

(*b*) *sex*, as the consumption patterns of men and women differ significantly, as, for example, in clothing;

(*c*) *socio-economic grouping*, by which society can be divided into levels broadly representing different levels of purchasing power. Membership of a socio-economic group has an important influence upon the types of product bought, for example, choice of a car or daily newspaper.

4. The purpose of marketing. The function of marketing is to get the product to the right place at the right time and to arrange the transfer of ownership from supplier to consumer. An organization in business must create *utility* for its consumers, and there are four forms of utility – form, time, place, and ownership.

(*a*) *Form utility* is created when raw materials are converted into finished products of good quality at reasonable price.

(*b*) *Time utility* entails having the finished product available for purchase by consumers when they require it.

(*c*) *Place utility* is created when the product appears in a location at which it can be purchased conveniently.

(*d*) *Ownership utility* comes about by arranging for the transfer of title from supplier to consumer.

5. The marketing concept. In previous times firms adopted a *product orientated* approach, producing those goods determined mainly by production considerations. Today, however, this has been replaced by *consumer orientation* as firms now find it essential to satisfy the demands of consumers. The production process has become considerably more complex by specialization and technological development, and by the extensive range of choice presented to consumers. This has resulted in producers and consumers becoming further apart in both time and distance, and thus marketing has become more important in ensuring that consumers obtain the goods and services they require and that the capacity of the production system is matched by the level of consumer demand.

The need to adopt a consumer orientated approach became

obvious in the 1950s as manufacturers sought a rapid turnover of durable consumer goods, and ease and convenience to consumers were emphasised. Today, advertising clearly lays this emphasis upon most goods and services, in both the private and public sectors, as it is now recognized that products have to be considered in terms of their acceptability to consumers.

Marketing research

6. Definition. Marketing research is the obtaining, recording, and evaluation of data relating to the marketing of goods and services. It includes a number of elements:

(*a*) market research, which is the measurement and analysis of the nature of the market;
(*b*) sales research, involving analysis of locations;
(*c*) product research, by which the quality of the product is analyzed;
(*d*) advertising research, to determine the effectiveness of promotion.

7. Purpose. The function of marketing research is to determine the nature and extent of demand which exists for a product. By discovering what the public wants and in what quantity, the right type of product can be produced to meet the demand. It is also important to assess the influences which motivate the public's choice of product, such factors as the optimum price, name, or packaging, for example.

8. Methods. Researchers use a variety of approaches to determine the important characteristics relating to their particular market. Many facts are readily available from published sources, for example, Government statistics on income, or sales figures for similar products. Typically, interviewers are employed to question members of the public, and questionnaires are used to ensure information can be gathered in an orderly manner and scientifically analyzed. Usually researchers depend upon sampling, i.e. contacting a cross-section of the public. Occasionally, *test-marketing* is employed, whereby a limited advertising campaign in a small locality aims to test public reaction to a new product prior to a national launch.

9. Forecasting. The next stage is that of attempting predictions based upon the results of market research. The effectiveness of such forecasting depends considerably upon the accuracy of the information gathered and its relevance to the whole market for the product. There will inevitably always remain the impossibilty of ensuring that all factors relating to the product's sales can be predicted with accuracy.

A variety of forms of forecasting may be used in business, such as Government assessments of economic trends, or a trade organization's evaluation of technological developments within an industry. Sales forecasts are commonly used to predict changing trends in demand, usually based upon sales figures for the product and estimates by sales staff of future trends.

10. Planning. The next stage is the application of intelligence obtained by research and forecasts made. A firm will now base its strategy upon its evaluation of expected consumer trends relating to its product. The marketing strategy becomes part of the firm's corporate plan, within which the various aspects of the organization can be united in seeking to achieve the goals of the firm in relation to its customers.

The marketing mix

11. Definition. When marketing research has identified the market for a particular product and distinguished any characteristics, the next stage is the strategy for ensuring the product meets the needs of consumers in that market. The strategy can be divided into four main aspects: product strategy; distribution strategy; pricing strategy; and promotional strategy. These four aspects together are known as the marketing mix, by which consumer demands are met and which ensures the success of the marketing strategy.

12. Product strategy. Product strategy is concerned with various aspects of the product itself: its life cycle, brand name, design, and form of packaging, etc.

(*a*) Product life-cycle. The sales figures of most products indicate that there is a definite pattern to their performance between the time of their introduction on to the market until they are withdrawn. This product life-cycle can be typically divided into four main phases, as seen in Fig. 7.1.

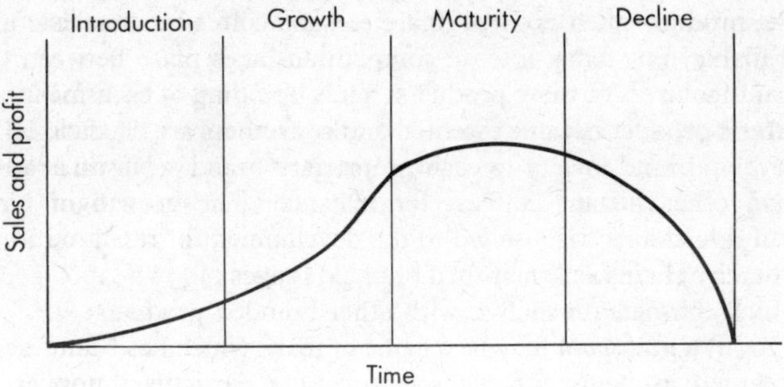

Figure 7.1 *Product life cycle*

(*i*) In the *introduction phase* a firm will spend heavily to promote its new product in order to bring it to the attention of as wide an area of the market as possible. This stage will probably involve capital investment in equipment and new staff, and sales may initially be disappointing in terms of the firm's outlay.

(*ii*) This stage is followed by a *growth stage* in which the product has become established, profits are earned, and the market continues to grow by established customers re-purchasing or by recommendations made to new customers.

(*iii*) *The maturity phase* follows in which the market may have become saturated and future development seems unlikely. Sales may decline as a result of competition and price-cutting from other producers.

(*iv*) The final *decline stage* will probably see a continuing fall in demand for the product and falling profits. Price-cutting may continue and there may be the innovation of a new product, for example, a change in fashion, which may drive the existing product out of the market.

(*b*) *Product identity*. A product may be distinquished from other similar products by such means as brand names, trade-marks, or packaging. It is very important in marketing to ensure that a product has an identity or 'image' as competition is frequently between very similar or standardized products which are mass-produced. Product identity can be achieved by:

(*i*) a *brand-name* for the particular product which is instantly recognizable to the public as being different to other similar products. In the early development of industrialization, for example, products such as soap, cigarettes, and coffee became generally available, but today intense competition takes place between the manufacturers of these products. Thus branding of each manufacturer's product became essential and consumers are encouraged to develop brand loyalty to each proprietary brand – Nescafé rather than other instant coffees, for instance. The growth of large multiple chains has also led to the development of retail branding whereby chains sell their own branded ranges of 'own-label' goods which compete on shelves with other branded products;

(*ii*) a *trademark* may be a name or mark which has been legally accepted as being for the sole use of a particular supplier or product. This affords a greater distinction for a product over others in the market, for example, the immediately recognizable McDonald's 'M' logo or specially designed names such as Kodak and Coca-Cola. The main legal requirement for the acceptance of a trademark is that it should be 'distinctive' and thus able to be distinquished from other similar brands or products.

(*c*) *Packaging*. The way a product is presented for sale to the market is also regarded as an important aspect of marketing. Today, so many different brands of a product may be located together on supermarket shelving that easily recognizable packaging of a product may be crucial in catching the attention of consumers.

13. Distribution strategy. The physical distribution of products is achieved by marketing channels organized by retailers and wholesalers. These are discussed in Chapter 9.

14. Pricing strategy. Pricing is a vital aspect of marketing strategy, and a product's success or failure depends largely upon the value placed upon it in the market by consumers. In a general sense, pricing is also important in determining how resources are allocated. A number of factors are involved in the determination of the price of a commodity, including the types of cost incurred in production; the nature of profit; and demand factors. These are discussed in Chapter 8.

All consumers have limited resources with which to make their purchases, and price therefore helps their decision-making regarding what products and brands to buy. In recent years there has been a great deal of price competition as large firms have been willing to cut costs and profit margins in order to win larger sectors of markets, and consumers have been encouraged to take advantage of a range of discounts and bargain offers. Consumers are also conscious of quality and tend to equate higher prices with better quality, which is obviously important in terms of marketing products which may be perceived as having an 'up-market' image.

15. Promotional strategy. Promotional strategy is the function of communication between the firm and the market by informing or persuading consumers in order to influence their decisions on purchases. It involves three aspects: personal selling; sales promotion; and advertising.

(*a*) *Personal selling* is the person-to-person approach between a member of a firm's sales force and a prospective customer. There is great variety in the nature of the selling function, which may be simple processing of regular orders, creative or persuasive selling of a new product, or even establishing the reputation of the firm and its products. Sales staff may often be employed in a technical capacity, responsible for briefing dealers on detailed specifications of a product, while large firms may have staff engaged upon relationship with 'key accounts', i.e. the firm's major customers. The importance of the selling function is normally recognized by the payment of commission of a percentage on sales obtained to sales staff in addition to basic salary.

(*b*) *Advertising* is the means by which the consumers' attention is drawn to a product so that information may be given and prospective customers are encouraged to buy. This is discussed more fully in the next section.

(*c*) *Sales promotion* consists of those elements of promotion other than advertising and personal selling, and which may support advertising campaigns. The 'point-of-sale' display or demonstration, for example, of a product at the location in a store where payment is made is often used for promoting a new product. A firm's name may be kept in the public's attention by free distribution of small items such as pens or calendars inscribed with the firm's name or its product. Similarly, samples of a product, if inexpensive, may be given to prospective purchasers in order to gain acceptance. Coupons included in advertisements which can be redeemed at a price discount when a product is bought can be an effective means of encouraging people to try out a new product. Trading stamps given with purchases can stimulate consumer loyalty to a particular product or brand.

Advertising

16. Introduction. Advertising is a form of sales presentation intended to bring products to the attention of prospective purchasers by using various media. Advertising has become an important industry in its own right as mass markets have appeared in most products and consumers have sought after goods which reflect improving standards of living.

17. Purpose of advertising. There are two main purposes in advertising:

(*a*) to *inform* the public, possibly about the launch of a new product, opening of a new store, or to make an announcement in the public interest, for example, urging energy saving or discouraging drinking and driving;

(*b*) to *persuade* consumers to buy, known as manufacturers' consumer advertising (MCA).

18. Methods of advertising. A variety of means are employed in advertising today, and cost and effectiveness have to be calculated carefully. *See* Fig. 7.2 for total expenditure on advertising in the UK.

19. Press. As can be seen from Fig. 7.2, more expenditure is made upon advertising in the press than upon any other medium. It is convenient to examine press advertising in two categories: newspapers and magazines.

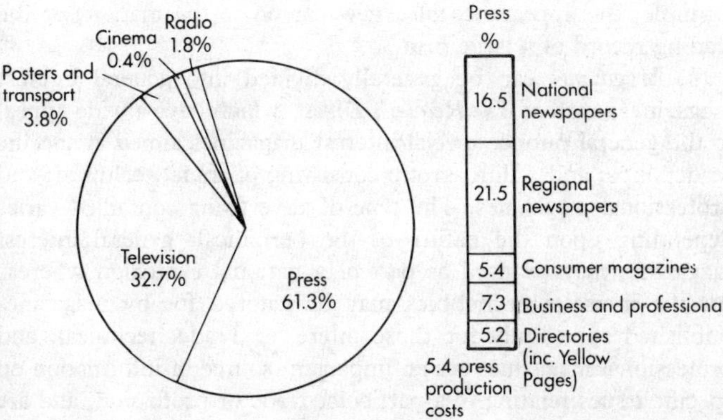

Figure 7.2 *Forms of advertising, 1986. Total advertising expenditure by media*

(*a*) *Newspapers* carry a wide range of advertising, and considerable progress has been made with the introduction of technological developments and especially with the use of colour. The type of advertisement carried depends to a large extent upon whether a newspaper is a local or regional newspaper, or a national daily or Sunday paper.

A greater proportion of advertising revenue is paid to local newspapers than to national dailies, probably reflecting the importance of local advertising by retailers and services. Much of the advertising carried by a local newspaper may be in the form of classified 'small-ads' for a diverse range of items such as property, household goods, cars, and holiday accommodation, all described very briefly and grouped together with similar items. Many local newspapers have a large proportion of their space taken up by advertisements, and there is a continuing trend towards the appearance of free local papers, the full cost of which is met by the advertisements carried, and which contain mostly advertising material.

The type of advertisement carried by a national daily newspaper will largely depend upon its readership. Dailies are classified generally into the mainly tabloid 'popular' press and the broadsheet 'quality' press. In addition to classified advertisements, there has been a recent trend towards large-scale advertising, such as full-page advertisements, often in colour, announcing, for example, the appearance of a new car on to the market, or the trading record of a large firm.

(*b*) *Magazines* can be generally divided into general interest magazines (such as *The Reader's Digest*) which have a wide appeal to the general public; special interest magazines aimed at specific readerships; and a third group consisting of trade, technical, and professional magazines. The type of advertising contained varies depending upon the nature of the periodical: general interest magazines may be used as part of a national campaign whereas specific interests or hobbies may be catered for by magazines published specifically for those interests. Trade, technical, and professional magazines are an important source of information on specific issues relating to a particular trade or profession, and are often the most important medium for notifying new developments or job vacancies.

20. Television. Commercial television was introduced to Britain in 1955, and is organized by the Independent Television Authority (ITA). TV companies are granted franchises to produce and broadcast programmes in 14 regions, for example, Thames TV serves the London area and Harlech covers Wales. Programmes are paid for from revenue raised from firms who buy 'slots' between programmes to show advertising films. Advertising time can be bought in units of from ten seconds upwards, and a maximum of six minutes in each hour is available to advertisers. Advertising time is extremely costly but these 'commercial breaks' obviously reach a wide audience, and considerable care and expense is expended upon producing advertisements. Charges for advertising are based upon time of transmission, and peak viewing time during the evening is very expensive. A strict code of conduct is operated by the ITA and is this discussed in Chapter 17.

To a large extent, advertising is now dominated by television. Television is a mass medium which offers the use of sound and vision, presentation in colour, and the association of a particular product with a catch-phrase or musical 'jingle'. The range of products advertised on television has been considerably extended since the early years of the medium. Initially, consumer products such as toiletries, petrol, and foodstuffs were the main items seen, but it has now become a more general medium, used to publicize services such as travel, holidays, banking, and insurance, as well as general retailing advertisements and government announcements.

21. Radio. Radio provides a largely supporting form of advertising, sponsors paying for regular commercial breaks which provide revenue for producing programmes. Radio advertising has been more popular in other countries such as the USA, although recent years have seen the development of many local commercial stations in Britain, such as Piccadilly Radio serving Manchester, and Capital Radio which broadcasts in the London region. Radio Luxembourg was for many years the only experience many people had of commercial radio. Radio provides a narrower market than television, consisting of people at home during the day, teenagers in the evenings, and motorists on their way to and from work. Radio advertising is subject, as with television, to the Independent Broadcasting Authority's (IBA) Code of Advertising Practice, and advertising time is limited to a maximum of nine minutes in any hour.

22. Cinema. Cinema advertising is no longer a significant form of advertising, as audiences have declined in the face of competition from television and the popularity of video hire. Most advertising in the cinema therefore targets products bought by teenagers and young adults who form the main proportion of cinema-goers today. It is essentially a localized form of advertising, used by local retailers, as well as for established products such as chocolates and toiletries, and services such as banking and insurance.

23. Outdoor advertising. *Outdoor* advertising using large hoardings on roadsides, posters in shopping centres, and signs erected at sporting events is a traditional form of advertising. Like radio, it is mainly a supporting form of advertising, often carrying only a simple mention of a brand name, a recognizable sign or picture, or a short message. It is intended to catch the attention of the passing motorist, passengers at railway station and underground subways, or shoppers moving between shops.

24. Direct response advertising. Direct response advertising, by which suppliers contact potential customers directly, is a rapidly expanding form of advertising. Lists of likely customers are bought by suppliers from agencies, and 'mail shots' of advertising materials can be sent personally to each one. The approach may be in the form of a telephone call to introduce a product – often double-glazing or kitchen fitments – with an invitation to take advantage of a bargain offer or to have a personal visit by the firm's representative. Television advertising is increasingly linked with direct selling, with customers invited to respond to an advertisement by telephoning to order a product advertised and to make payment at the same time by credit card. See 9:**11** for more detail of direct selling.

25. Advertising techniques. A variety of different approaches is available to advertisers. It has already been noted that the media is used for differing purposes: newspapers or television are used to convey a lengthy and persuasive message about a product while radio and roadside hoardings might serve only to remind consumers of that product. Technique and method of approach will be determined by the product and the type of image the product wishes to create in the minds of consumers. Thus an advertising campaign will frequently seek to associate a product with an image of success, envy, admiration, or the 'good life'. Many brands of margarine, for example, communicate an image of health and vitality, while advertisements for beer emphasise the warmth and friendliness of the British 'pub'. Romance and glamour are also held to be desirable images, for example, in advertising chocolates or toiletries, and the testimony of a well-known public figure is often used to lend greater credibility to a product. The launch of a new product frequently involves the 'hard sell' by which advertisers claim superlatives such as 'better', 'greater', 'cheaper', or 'bigger' for their product over that of rivals.

26. Advertising agencies. Advertising is held to be of such importance today that a large proportion of the total expenditure is spent by specialist advertising agencies acting on behalf of clients. Advertising agencies are able to provide clients with a wide range of promotional and public relations expertise, and act as the link between clients and the media. Clients – referred to as 'accounts' – pay fees to the agency for whatever marketing research may be necessary, and for production of the advertising campaign. Agencies receive their main income in the form of commission from the media with whom they place their clients' advertising campaign. There has been a considerable growth of advertising agencies in recent years, many now becoming international companies, and the accounts of large companies give rise to intense competition between agencies.

About 90 per cent of advertising placed by agencies in Britain is handled by those who are members of the Institute of Practitioners in Advertising (IPA) which ensures professional standards of behaviour. The Advertising Association provides a forum for advertisers, agencies, and the media in order to promote public confidence in advertising.

27. Advantages of advertising. Advertising brings about

(*a*) increase in sales and therefore larger quantities produced, thus affording cheaper goods by the economies of scale;

(*b*) awareness of new products and developments by consumers;

(*c*) stimulation of product development;

(*d*) increased revenue for media, for example by supporting television programmes and sporting events.

28. Criticisms of advertising

(*a*) Advertising is obviously costly and advertisers can be accused of being wasteful of resources.

(*b*) It can become increasingly costly as competitors are forced to advertise to counter advertising by rival firms.

(*c*) The boring and repetitive nature of many advertisements and 'jingles'.

(*d*) People can be persuaded to live beyond their means.

(*e*) Advertisements may mislead by over-emphasising only a product's good points and omitting defects.

(*f*) Control and legislation has on occasion been found necessary to curb advertising which may be offensive or dangerous.

29. Control of advertising. The need for control over advertising in Britain has largely been met by self-discipline within the advertising industry and is discussed in Chapter 17.

Case 7 The launch of Biarritz

The market for boxed chocolates has been fairly static in recent years. Demand is fairly constant throughout the year until the exceptional peak at the end of the year when boxes of chocolates become Christmas presents – between 50 and 55 per cent of total sales take place within the two months of November and December. The market is dominated by the products of three main firms – Cadbury's, Rowntree's, and Terry's – who between them produce about 90 per cent of the total supply, the remainder being supplied by smaller firms such as Thornton's, foreign suppliers, and some produced as own brands for shops.

Cadbury's decided that there was a gap in the market which a new brand of plain assorted chocolates might fill. Four possible new options were proposed and a market research agency employed to examine their feasibility. An independent view was thus obtained for Cadbury's, on the basis of testing in a simulated shop environment to evaluate people's responses to the new lines. Results seemed to be positively in favour of one proposed new brand, and the decision was taken to put it into production.

Market research had indicated that the market – traditionally rather conservative – was ripe for innovation. Because boxes of chocolates are so often given as gifts, it was decided that packaging was a vital aspect of marketing. The traditional square box was therefore rejected and the new product gained its main distinctive feature – a new triangular shaped box. To go with its modern packaging a name which would convey an impression of style and sophistication was chosen – Biarritz.

The launch of Biarritz took place in September 1986. An advertising agency – Gold, Greenlees, and Trott – had been commissioned to promote the new product. The main medium used to promote confectionary products is TV, and an advertising feature had been made in readiness for the launch. The advertisement was shown widely in the important pre-Christmas period, laying emphasis upon how sophisticated it was to both give and receive Biarritz, and creating a highly distinctive image which the public would recognize as being different to other chocolates on the market.

Results to date seem to have borne out Cadbury's belief in

Biarritz which is now firmly established in the market. The market for plain assorted boxed chocolates itself has grown, and much of the growth has been as a result of new business stimulated by the introduction of Biarritz – people who might otherwise not have been tempted to buy chocolates.

Progress test 8

1. What is marketing? (**1**)
2. What do you understand by 'market segmentation'? (**3**)
3. What is the purpose of marketing? (**4**)
4. Discuss the marketing concept.(**5**)
5. What is marketing research? (**6**)
6. How is it conducted? (**8**)
7. What is the 'marketing mix'? (**11**)
8. Describe a typical product life-cycle. (**12**)
9. Discuss product identity. (**12**)
10. Briefly describe promotional strategy (**15**)
11. What is advertising? (**16**)
12. Describe the main methods of advertising. (**18–24**)
13. Discuss advertising techniques. (**25**)
14. What is the role of advertising agencies? (**26**)
15. What are the advantages and disadvantages of advertising? (**27,28**)
16. How did Cadbury's test the market for Biarritz? (**Case 7**)
17. Describe how Biarritz was launched. (**Case 7**)

8

Production

Introduction

1. Definition. Production is the means whereby resources are organized to produce the goods and services which people require. Services, as well as goods, are included in the definition, as the purpose of production is the satisfaction of wants, and in today's world an increasing number of people are employed in service industries such as banking, leisure, finance, and administration.

2. Factors of production. In order to achieve production, four inputs or *factors of production* are normally necessary.

(*a*) *Land*: regarded as a 'gift of nature' and including any valuable mineral deposits. It is the basic requirement of space within which factories may be sited, foodstuffs grown, or services provided.

(*b*) *Labour*: an essential element in all forms of production. It represents all forms of work or human effort, both manual and mental.

(*c*) *Capital*: in the economic sense, capital may be defined as goods used to produce other goods. Property such as a factory building, machinery such as robots for welding car bodies, and raw materials such as textiles to be made into clothes are all forms of capital to be used in the process of production.

(*d*) *Enterprise*: defined as being the organizational skills of combining the factors of production in the most effective proportion to ensure maximum levels of production. The person in whom this skill is found – the entrepreneur – has traditionally been the owner of an enterprise who has developed a business by combining the functions of decision-making and risk-taking. In large firms, however, it is difficult to define the entrepreneur – shareholders take the risk of investing money in the business but decisions are taken by executives who are paid a salary.

3. Combination of factors. In order to ensure that factors are used to their maximum effectiveness and that production is maximized from the available resources, an organization has to calculate the optimum combination of factors used. Increases in output, however, may not be produced directly in proportion to increases in inputs of factors of production.

(*a*) The *law of diminishing returns* shows how increasing inputs may lead to non-proportional returns. It states that if increasing quantities of one factor (e.g. labour) are used with a fixed quantity of another factor (e.g. land) output will eventually decrease. This can be understood by thinking of the effect upon production of having more farm workers in a field of a certain size, or of having an increasing number of factory workers in a small workshop. Initially, additional workers may increase production up to a point at which the correct combination of land and labour will achieve maximum output, but beyond a certain point the disproportionate number of workers for the field or workshop will cause output to fall. The amount each new additional worker produces – the 'marginal product' will start to fall and is followed by a fall in 'average product' (i.e. of all the workers). Finally, the 'total product' of the entire workforce begins to decline. The theory simply notes the relationship between the factors of production and cannot determine how many units of a factor will be employed as this will have to be based on factor cost.

(*b*) The question of whether a factor is *fixed* or *variable* depends upon whether production takes place in the short run or the long run.

(*i*) The *short run* (or short term) is defined as being a period of time during which the amount of some factors cannot be increased. If, for example, we think of a typical factory, the building itself would have to be regarded as *fixed*, as extending the building or erecting a new and larger building would probably be a fairly lengthy process. Thus the time during which the premises, and therefore possibly the machinery it houses, could not be enlarged would be the short run – capital in this case is the fixed factor whilst other factors, such as labour, could, of course be *varied*.

(*ii*) The *long run* can be defined as being a period of time during which the input of all factors can be varied. In addition to more or less labour being employed as in the short run, in the long run (or long term) new buildings could be erected and the amount of equipment increased.

4. Types of production. There are three main forms of production: primary, secondary, and tertiary.

(*a*) *Primary*: includes a wide range of occupations directly involved in obtaining ores from the earth, crops from the land, or fish from the sea.

(*b*) *Secondary*: in which materials are changed into products for consumption or further use, e.g. the factory manufacture of goods or the refining of iron ore into steel.

(*c*) *Tertiary*, or the provision of services. Distinction may be made between direct services, such as teaching, and indirect services, such as banking.

In recent years a fourth form – *quarternary* – has emerged, in which can be included the fast developing leisure industries such as sport.

5. Production decisions. The main decisions to be made by a society in order to maximize production from limited resources are:

(*a*) What to produce? Limited resources dictate that choices have to be made between conflicting demands.

(*b*) How to produce? Should production be *labour-intensive*, with most tasks performed by workers, or *capital-intensive*, with fewer workers using sophisticated machinery?

(*c*) For whom to produce? Society has to ensure the efficient working of a system for the distribution of goods and services.

How these questions are decided depends largely upon the

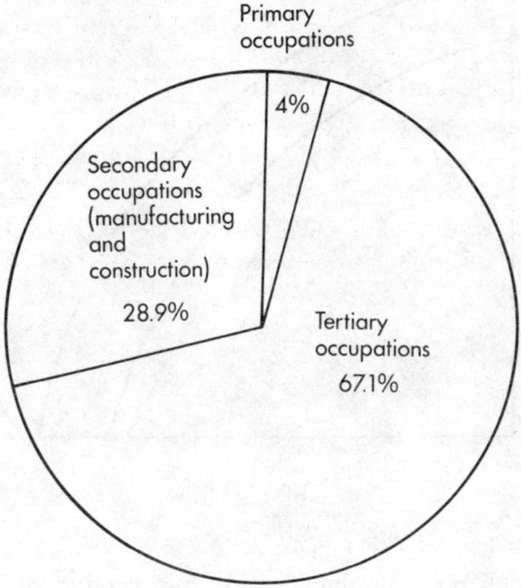

Figure 8.1 *Forms of production (by employment, 1986)*

economic system of the country (*see* 1:7). In free-market economies, the price mechanism is generally responsible for allocating resources, determining what methods of production are used, and how goods are distributed. In command economies production decisions, as well as allocation of goods are made by the state, as it is the state which owns the means of production and distribution. The choices facing a society are shown in Fig 8.2.

In the diagram, it is assumed that the country produces only two types of product – clothing and steel. As the resources for making the products are limited, the amount of clothing, for example, can only be increased by withdrawing inputs from the production of steel – the *opportunity cost* of producing more of one product is the amount of the other which has been lost. The *production possibility curve* (PP) shows how much of each product can be made by using all the available resources. The decision could be made to produce only clothing and no steel, in which case production would be at point *A*. Alternatively, point *B* shows that production could be at a point where only steel would be produced. The probable decision would be to produce an accep-

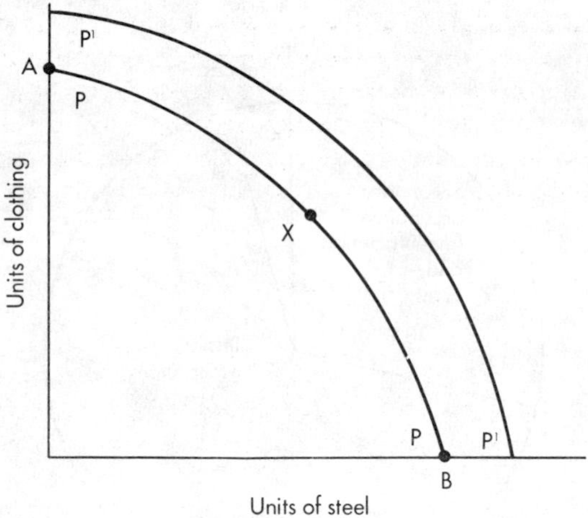

Figure 8.2 *Production possibility curve*

table level of both products, and thus production would be somewhere to the middle of the production possibility curve possibly at *X*.

Production anywhere inside the curve would mean that available resources were not fully utilized. If, however, the country's stock of resources were increased, then production possibilities would be increased – as shown by the new production possibility curve P^1-P^1 indicating new production levels of clothing and steel.

The scale of production

6. Returns to scale. It is important that a firm seeks to achieve an *optimum* level of output at which costs are lowest. A firm has to decide upon what scale to produce, as costs change as the level of production is increased or decreased. If output increases in the same proportion as the increase in inputs of factors of production then the firm is said to be achieving *constant returns to scale*. It is possible that at some stage of production the firm may find that increases in inputs results in a less than proportionate increase in output and in this case there is said to be *decreasing returns to scale*. It is more usual, however, for firms to find that as inputs are increased and the scale of production becomes larger it begins to achieve *increasing returns to scale*. Business experience would seem to indicate that firms seek growth, for example by mergers and take-overs, in order that production on a larger scale would result in lower costs per item of production. The reasons why large-scale production may result in lower costs are known as the *economies of scale*.

7. Economies of scale. The benefits of large-scale production, or economies of scale, may be examined as *internal* economies of scale, and as *external* economies of scale.

8. Internal economies of scale. These are economies which a firm achieves when the scale of its production is increased, and may result from the following:

(a) *Technical economies*, which may arise from the use of new machinery or techniques which could not be used at a lower level of production:

(*i*) Increased output might allow more *specialization* and application of the principle of the *division of labour* (*see* 1:5). Highly specialized equipment might be brought in to perform specific tasks, and workers engaged upon a single aspect become highly specialized and proficient. This is the basis of most modern production lines in large industries.

(*ii*) An increase in the size of the production unit might increase production without the need for further inputs of factors. A number of oil tankers, for example, have been lengthened to carry a larger volume of oil but can be handled by the same number of crew members. In many industries such as car manufacturing or steel refining, the nature of the process makes large-scale organization the only viable form of production.

(*iii*) Large-scale production often results in machines and equipment being used more intensively, e.g. by shift-working.

(*iv*) An increase in output may result in the development of sub-industries, e.g. waste products from a large plant may be of sufficient quantity to merit separate processing into usable products, e.g. fire-lighters from wood-shavings in the furniture industry.

(*b*) *Managerial economies* arise from the increased scope for the division of labour in the administration of a firm. Whereas a small firm may require management to fill a number of roles, a large firm can employ specialists. Thus expertise may be obtained and distinction made between various functions such as sales, production, finance, and marketing (*see* 6:**6**).

(*c*) *Financial economies* occur because large firms are regarded as a safer investment than smaller companies and are therefore in a better position to raise capital. Thus the assets of a large company will inspire confidence in investors who may be able to buy and sell its shares on the Stock Exchange. Banks will be willing to make loans at a more favourable rate of interest than to a smaller firm because of the security provided.

(*d*) *Commercial economies* may exist when a large firm is able to buy supplies of raw materials in bulk at lower cost. Similarly, a large firm's marketing operation may be cheaper than that of a small firm as it can consign and distribute products in bulk. Other advantages often accrue, e.g. transport may be cheaper on a large scale, and the firm may be able to increase sales by extensive advertising.

(*e*) *Risk-bearing economies* result from a large organization's capacity to obtain supplies from a wide range of sources and likewise to diversify its output and its markets. Large-scale organizations in such industries as tea or coffee producing, for example, will obtain supplies from a number of different countries, while many large international companies, because of their varied activities, are able to diversify into more profitable areas of production as market trends change.

9. External economies of scale. These may arise due to the development of the industry in which a firm produces. Such developments tend to benefit all firms in the industry, both large and small. External economies may be as a result of economies of information; as a result of concentration; and those resulting from disintegration.

(*a*) *Information* on all aspects of business relating to the firm may prove valuable. Such information as market conditions and financial assistance, for example, may be provided by the industry's own association or by the government.

(*b*) *Concentration* of an industry in a particular area may result in the firms in that industry achieving various economies. Improvements to the infrastructure of the area may mean better transport facilities, for example, and other services such as banking which may be common to many companies may develop as a result. Firms providing specialist services or products for the industry may be attracted to the area, and the existence of a skilled labour force may be supported by training and educational facilities.

(*c*) *Disintegration* of an industry may occur as that industry grows. The car industry, for example, at one time developed into specialist sectors, each sector producing components for major firms by themselves enjoying the benefits of large-scale production.

10. Diseconomies of scale. Despite the many advantages which may occur as a result of the growth of larger organizations, certain disadvantages may also appear.

(*a*) Internal diseconomies of scale sometimes appear as growth can so affect an organization that it becomes difficult to manage effectively. Communications may prove difficult in a more unwieldy organization and decision-making may be harder to effect. Morale can become difficult to maintain and the work-force may feel alienated from management.

(*b*) External diseconomies of scale may develop for a number of reasons. Concentration of an industry in an area may lead to that area's over-dependence upon it and to the danger of collapse of the local economy in the event of recession in the industry. The social costs of an industry in an area may provoke public opposition, e.g. against pollution, and there may be excessive demand upon housing and services such as education and health.

11. Growth and integration. The aim of business is to increase profits and the possibility of securing economies of scale will encourage the growth of firms. Growth will normally be achieved by integration in several ways.

(*a*) *Horizontal integration*, whereby firms at the same stage of production amalgamate, frequently by merger or take-over. The advantages expected, for example, in some of the mergers of retailing organizations in recent times, include lower costs because of economies of scale in administration, and a larger share of the market by reducing competition. Government action against monopoly power resulting from mergers may be taken in the public interest (*see* 17:**9**)

(*b*) *Vertical integration* occurs when firms engaged in different stages of production amalgamate. Integration may be either backward or forward. In backward integration a firm may take control of suppliers of materials or components, for example, tea or coffee firms may buy up plantations in order to ensure control over supplies. Forward integration may take place when firms obtain control over distribution networks to ensure an outlet for their products, for example, breweries gaining control of public houses.

(*c*) Lateral integration takes place when firms producing different goods amalgamate. It is hoped that risks such as changes in fashion may be spread over a wider product range and reduce reliance upon a single product. This form of integration gives rise to conglomerates, such as the Rank Organisation, which control a wide range of diverse activities.

12. The small firm. Despite the advantages of large-scale production, the small firm remains an important unit at all levels of production. Some small firms may, of course, be in an early stage of development, but there are a number of reasons to explain the continued existence of some firms as small units.

(*a*) The market may be limited, for example, for designer clothes or antique jewellery; localized such as a bakery or village shop; or restricted by transport as with perishable foodstuffs.

(*b*) The nature of the industry may be more suitable to smaller scale production, e.g. many service industries such as tailoring or hairdressing in which individual tastes may be catered for, or large industries such as motor manufacturing which may be subject to disintegration.

(*c*) Lack of capital may prevent development.

(*d*) Management (often the sole owner of the enterprise) may prefer to remain on a small scale, or lack of expertise may restrict development.

(*e*) Many firms maintain their small size by co-operating with others, as, for example, in retailing where small village shops are able to achieve economies of scale by membership of organizations such as Mace and Spar.

Costs of production

13. Costs. The term *opportunity-cost* explains that the real cost of deciding upon expenditure on one item is the alternative of spending on other items we have to forego. In business, costs are incurred in the normal course of activity and have to be calculated in order to ensure the efficient running of the enterprise. There are several types of costs.

(*a*) *Fixed costs* are costs incurred whether production is taking place or not. Sometimes referred to as 'overheads' they include the cost of premises, rents, rates, equipment, interest payments on loans, and depreciation of equipment. Fixed costs can, of course, be varied in the long run (*see* **3**(b)) in response to changing circumstances, for example, the need for larger or smaller premises.

(*b*) *Variable costs* are those costs which vary with output and include items such as labour, raw materials, and fuel. As output increases, the cost of the various factors rises, possibly slowly at first because of economies of scale but then increasing rapidly as the optimum production level is passed.

(*c*) *Total costs* are the combined total of fixed and variable costs.

(*d*) *Average (or unit) costs* enable a firm to calculate the cost of each unit of their production by dividing total costs by the number of units produced. As both fixed and variable costs are included, average costs will be high at an early stage of production because of the effect of fixed costs, but normally begin to fall with increased output as fixed costs become proportionately lower. Average costs indicate to the producer the optimum level of production at the point of lowest unit cost.

(*e*) *Marginal cost* is the cost incurred in the production of an additional unit, and is simply the addition to total cost made by that 'extra' unit. It is an important concept for the businessman, as the point where marginal and average costs coincide will be seen as being capacity output from existing factors of production.

Figure 8.3 shows marginal cost and average cost curves drawn from a firm's cost schedules. Average cost and marginal cost are equal at the lowest point of the average cost curve, and this indicates capacity output.

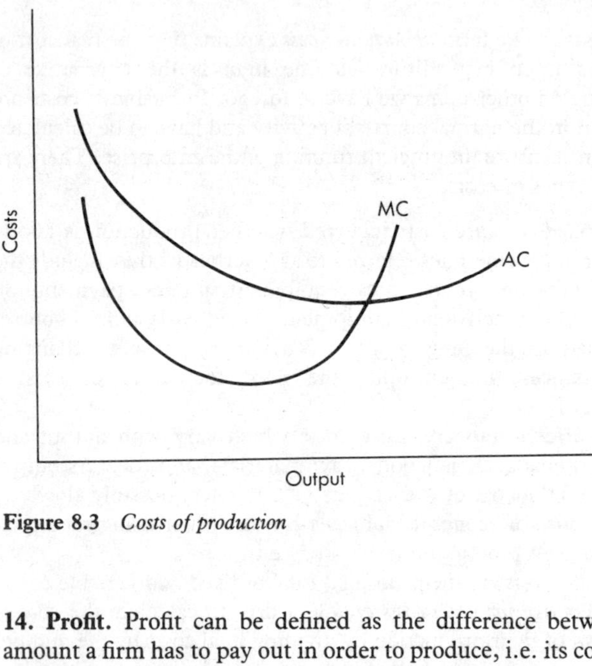

Figure 8.3 *Costs of production*

14. Profit. Profit can be defined as the difference between the amount a firm has to pay out in order to produce, i.e. its costs, and the amount it receives for that production of goods or services, i.e. its revenue. Profit includes two elements – a return on the risk taken with capital, and the opportunity-cost of the money which could have been placed in alternative use.

Normal profit can be regarded as the cost to the firm necessary to ensure that the firm is able to remain in the existing line of business, i.e. a level of profit below which capital would be moved out of the firm into a more profitable use. Normal profit is therefore included as a cost of production, so that a firm in which average cost is equal to average revenue is making normal profits. Any profit earned above this level of normal profit is referred to as *supernormal profit.*

Case 8 Production of the Rover 800

Although Austin Rover is a small producer by international car manufacturing standards, its two main manufacturing plants at Longbridge and Cowley have some of the most advanced technology in the world. Whereas car manufacturing has traditionally depended upon large-scale production lines building a continuous stream of identical models, the introduction of robots into most stages of production now gives the industry flexibility to provide the consumer with a range of optional models.

The Rover 800 series was developed in collaboration with the Japanese manufacturer, Honda. Austin Rover builds both the Rover 800 and its sister car, the Honda Legend, while the model is sold in the USA badged as Sterling. The production of the 800 series has seen the application of some of the most up-to-date manufacturing technologies in the world, using robots for a wide range of sophisticated tasks.

The first stage in bringing the Rover 800 into being was the design stage, in which a full-size, three-dimensional clay model was made of the car. From this model, measurements were made which were then stored in the computer and became the 'master database' for all future work on the car. In the pre-production stage, press tools for the 400 body panels and assembly tools were designed and made, using computer controlled equipment, drawing information from the master database.

The body assembly facilities at Cowley are highly automated and flexible – although there are only four basic body types, 181 derivatives can be made in any sequence on the production line. The main parts – understructure, side panels, and roof – come together in a fully robotic body framing station in which 'gates' ensure the body is correctly positioned for welding. Over 4,000 welds are applied in the building process, almost a half by the 51 robots in service, and, after inspection, the body has doors, bonnet, and tailgate.

The car is then moved to the paint shop, where it is dipped and sprayed in a number of stages to prepare it for painting and finishing. Automated seam sealing takes place before the cars receive firstly a primer paint and then finally spraying in a variety of colours – again by robots.

The last stage is the trim and final assembly. An unusual feature of the Rover 800 construction is the removal of doors at this stage for fitting of locks, handles, and trim, which also allows easier access for completing the interior. Windscreen and rear window are fitted by robot, before the car is finally taken for computerized testing, including 'rolling road' testing to check such factors as braking, engine performance, gearbox effectiveness, and speedometer accuracy.

A vital aspect of the production of the 800 series is the emphasis upon quality. Throughout the building of the car, automated laser techniques constantly check the specifications of the car, while the commitment of employees is encouraged by greater involvement in such ways as testing and quality control.

Progress test 8

1. Define production. (**1**)
2. What are the factors of production? (**2**)
3. Discuss how factors may be combined. (**3**)
4. What do you understand by the term *diminishing returns*? (**3**)
5. What are the main types of production? (**4**)
6. What decisions have to be taken to maximize production? (**5**)
7. Describe what you understand by *production possibility*. (**5**)
8. Explain *returns to scale*. (**6**)
9. What internal economies of scale may be achieved? (**8**)
10. What are external economies of scale? (**9**)
11. What diseconomies might exist? (**10**)
12. Describe why small firms may continue to exist. (**12**)
13. What are the main costs faced by a firm? (**13**)
14. What is profit? Explain normal and supernormal profits. (**13**)
15. Briefly note the main stages in car production. (**Case 8**)
16. Discuss the importance of robotics in building the Rover 800. (**Case 8**)

9

Distribution

Introduction

1. Definition. Distribution is the means by which goods and services find their way from producers to consumers. It is a vital aspect of marketing, ensuring that products reach the consumer in the right place and at the right time. Thus the function of distribution contributes to the value of the product and provides the means by which ownership of it is transferred from producer to consumer. In addition, distribution is an important part of the service sector, providing employment for a wide range of people within the distribution network.

2. Channels of distribution. The means of physical distribution of goods and services are constantly changing, depending upon the nature of the market and consumers' needs. The two main forms of distribution are retailing and wholesaling, but within these two divisions there are many variations. Goods and services are now often distributed directly to the consumer by producers, whilst in many cases the scale of the distribution function is changing with many retail outlets becoming very large-scale.

Retailing

3. Introduction. Retailers are the final link in the distribution network. Retailers usually have direct contact with the consumer and as a result the many changes seen in retailing reflect the changing nature of consumer tastes and habits. The retail structure is constantly changing as newer forms of distribution appear and older forms disappear or are modified. Retailers are always diversifying products in order to maintain or increase their market share.

4. Functions. Retailers fulfil a number of important functions:

(*a*) they provide the producer with an outlet for goods and services;
(*b*) they provide consumers with a convenient source of goods and services;
(*c*) they provide the consumer with choice from a wide range of products;
(*d*) they are often a useful source of advice for consumers;
(*e*) they are a source of feedback to producers on sales and trends;
(*f*) they frequently provide services such as delivery and maintenance.

Types of retailing

5. Introduction. Because of the constantly changing nature of the retailing trade it is often difficult to distinguish between the various forms of outlet. The main types include the small, independent shop, the larger-scale multiple store and department store, and the enormous hypermarket. Also included are the stores of the Co-operative Retail Society, mail order organizations, various forms of direct selling, and vending machines.

6. The sole (independent) retailer. Many retail outlets are owned and operated by the owner – street market traders; mobile shops; and the small corner shop or general village store (often referred to as a 'unit' shop). The small shop has been a traditional feature of retailing in Britain, but numbers have declined in recent years as a result of competition from larger stores.

There are a number of reasons for the popularity of small shops:

(*a*) they provide personal attention for customers, for example by stocking brands of goods popular with their customers, or by the personal attention provided by the owner and assistant at a hairdressing salon, for instance;

(*b*) customers frequently appreciate the convenience of a shop nearby, often catering for a small neighbourhood or even a street;

(*c*) the costs of operating a small shop are usually lower as they are normally situated away from the main shopping centres.

Many small shops have become members of voluntary chains such as the grocery shops of Mace and Spar, formed as an association of independent retailers which are able to buy in bulk and so reduce costs. They were formed in order to combat the competition from larger businesses which has forced the closure of many small shops in recent years. Voluntary chains have been able to develop a corporate image by advertising and by standardising shop fittings and stock carried. Many small retail shops have survived as a result of membership of a voluntary chain and are able to keep the identity and control of the business.

7. **Department stores.** The department store is also a traditional form of retailing, usually in town and city centres where its many departments are housed on a number of floors of one building. They became popular at the turn of the century when the needs of the wealthy middle class had to be met and customer satisfaction was the main aim. Apart from their occupying prime sites, most department stores provided facilities such as tea-rooms and car-parks for customers and were usually heavily staffed by assistants. They have suffered as a result of the competition from large retail chains which in many cases have bought stores, for example, Harrods became part of the House of Fraser group and Brown's of Chester is owned by Debenhams. Their decline has been mainly as a result of social changes whereby today everyone is a consumer and more conscious of choices and price available, and thus larger chains able to cut prices have been able to dominate markets.

8. **Multiple (chain) stores.** A multiple store is a large organization, usually found nationally, which has at least ten branches. Multiples have enjoyed considerable growth as consumers have enjoyed economic prosperity, by buying in bulk, and by standardization of products and store layout. Most shopping centres are now dominated by the identical frontages of large multiples and the

consumer is attracted by the guarantee of known levels of quality and price.

Two main types of chain stores can be distinquished:

(*a*) *Specialist* chain stores which sell only one type of product, for example, shoes (Lilley & Skinner), jewellery (Ratners); and photographic equipment (Greens), and

(*b*) *Variety* chain stores, such as Woolworths, Marks & Spencer, and Littlewoods which sell a wide range of products. In recent years some specialist chains have moved into this category by widening their product range – W.H. Smith, for example, was originally purely a bookseller and stationer.

Together with the development of chain stores has been the increase in the size of shops, from supermarket to superstore and hypermarket (see below).

9. Co-operative retail societies. Most 'Co-op' stores resemble variety chain stores by occupying prime shopping centre positions and by selling a wide range of merchandise. The co-operative movement developed mainly through retail societies, which were non profit-making associations established to provide good quality merchandise at reasonable prices, but have found themselves having to compete with other retail organizations. Originally, retail societies were local, but the need to compete with large-scale retailers has made amalgamations and other changes essential, and today many stores are owned by Co-operative Retail Services. The establishment of a national image has been another development, especially by the 'Co-op' logo. (*See* 4:**16** for detail on Co-operative organization.)

10. Mail order. Supplying customers by post with goods chosen from catalogues has a long tradition. In Britain, as in many other parts of the world, mail order buying means that people in remote communities are able to be supplied with a variety of goods, especially clothing and footwear. In Britain, part-time agents usually call on customers – often friends or neighbours – who are invited to make choices from expensively produced catalogues. The mail order firm receives orders from agents and then sends goods direct to the customers. The customer pays a deposit and an agreed weekly sum to the agent, and payments are usually on a continuing basis rather than for one specific item. The agent receives commission – normally ten per cent. Prices are usually competitive as costs of retail premises, staff, and equipment are avoided. Goods are dispatched to purchasers promptly and can be returned if the customer is not satisfied with them.

In Britain, mail order buying enjoyed popularity in tightly-knit working-class communities, but has declined with increasing prosperity and the competition of other forms of retailing. It is, however, regarded as a form of retailing with potential, and the introduction of the Next Directory in 1988 indicates the possibility of renewed interest. The market is dominated by a few large firms, such as Great Universal Stores and Littlewoods. In addition to the traditional form of mail order firm supplying a wide range of goods, there are specialist firms supplying products such as books and records.

11. Direct selling. Direct selling (or *direct response marketing*), by which producers supply customers directly, by-passing retailers, is a rapidly developing form of marketing. The main forms are door-to-door selling, advertisements in newspapers and magazines, television and radio advertisements, and telephone calls and letters to prospective customers. The Post Office, by its ownership of the means of communication, is heavily involved in direct mail marketing, and provides services such as Freepost, the Business Reply Service, and rebates for large volumes of mail to its customers. In order to make each 'mail shot' effective, lists of suitable clients can be bought from agencies, and correspondence can refer individually to each prospective customer. A similar approach is made by firms selling products such as double-glazing whereby the firm's salespeople telephone prospective customers directly at home to introduce themselves and their product.

Television advertisements inviting consumers to buy a product by telephoning an order directly are increasing, especially as payment is made easier by use of credit cards. The possibilities for 'home shopping' by use of television advertisements in conjunction with computer facilities to enable choices to be made and payments transacted now exist. Experiments have already been carried out in communities where a local supermarket lists products on television, using Prestel, and customers place orders by using a computer keyboard.

Party selling is another form of direct selling, in which an organiser arranges for a hostess to hold a party for friends at which he or she will be present with samples. Sales are taken by the organiser and purchasers receive delivery of goods directly, and the host receives commission based upon sales made at the party. Products such as kitchen equipment (Tupperware), cosmetics (Avon), and lingerie (Pippa Dee) have proved suitable for this type of marketing.

12. Vending machines. For many types of consumer goods, vending machines provide a very suitable method of retailing. Cigarettes and sweets have long been available from machines in places where it might not have been possible to provided manned shops and kiosks, for example, at railway stations and airports where there may be round-the-clock demand. Recently, far more use is being made of vending machines to sell drinks such as coffee, tea, and soft drinks, and foodstuffs such as sandwiches.

Retailing trends

13. Large-scale retailing. Recent years have seen a continuous growth in the size of retail outlets. The number of small corner shops serving the needs of local communities has slowly declined, to be replaced by large stores providing for a much larger population. There are a number of reasons for this development:

(*a*) the increasing adoption of the *self-service* principle whereby goods are displayed and customers invited to make purchases and to pay at a central cash desk. This system has gradually displaced shops in which assistants were employed to supply purchasers with goods upon request;

(*b*) the public now seem to favour 'one-stop shopping', preferring to obtain all their needs in one extended visit to one location, rather than in isolated visits to shops for specific purchases.

(*c*) consumer spending has risen as people have the money to obtain goods formerly thought of as luxury items. In Britain, over

60 per cent of Gross Domestic Product is made up of consumer expenditure;

(*d*) multiple chains have gradually increased their proportion of retail expenditure and have found it cost-effective to build larger premises;

(*e*) traffic congestion in town centres has made 'out-of-town' locations desirable. Cheaper land and more space has made it possible to create larger stores with car-parking facilities and services such as petrol stations to attract customers.

The trend to larger-scale retail outlets has taken various different forms.

(*a*) The *supermarket* was the first implementation of the self-service principle, mainly retailing essential items of foodstuffs and household products. By definition, a supermarket has to occupy 2,500 square feet, and is usually found in shopping centres or on high streets. Many small independent retailers adopted the supermarket idea, and found that savings were possible by reduction in the number of staff needed, and as a result were able to retail goods to customers more cheaply. Many supermarkets are now in multiple organization, for example, by firms such as Fine Fare, or are part of voluntary chains such as Spar or Mace.

(*b*) The *superstore* became the next stage in the move towards large-scale retailing, as even larger premises were sought on the outskirts of towns. Most were owned by multiples, such as Asda, and their popularity brought about the closure of many town-centre supermarkets. Superstores offered a wider range of goods, such as furniture, clothing, electrical products, and do-it-yourself materials, in addition to foodstuffs and household goods.

(*c*) The *hypermarket* has been a logical development of the move towards larger scale retailing, and is defined as being an out-of-town store covering at least 23,000 square feet of selling area on one level. First developed in the USA and in Europe, the hypermarket is a complete shopping centre under one roof, stocking an extensive range of goods and services. The advantages of being able to wheel trolleys around displays on one floor, of having a number of convenient check-out points for payment, and easy access to car-parking have all contributed to the continuing popularity of hypermarkets. In Britain, the first hypermarket was opened by Carrefour at Caerphilly in South Wales in the early 1970s.

14. Town centre retailing. Retailing in the traditional town centres and high streets has sought to meet the competition of large out-of-town hypermarkets by various means.

(*a*) The main development has been the pedestrian *shopping precinct* in which many shops are housed within one building complex, such as Birmingham's Bull Ring or Manchester's Arndale Centre. These shopping centres have transformed the centres of most towns and cities, providing consumers with all major retail outlets under one roof in pleasantly designed surroundings with escalators for access to different levels, rest areas, all within reach of transport facilities.

(*b*) Developments are also taking place in the design of town centre stores to meet the changing demands of consumers. Many large department stores occupying prime central positions within towns are being transformed into small shopping centres by dividing up the store into small specialty shops. This is based upon the 'Galleria' concept similar to developments in the USA and Italy, aiming to attract consumers to an integrated collection of specialty shops under one roof. This development is an extension of the practice in recent years of more floor space in large stores being taken up by concessions such as Green's (electrical), and Wedgewood (china).

15. Lifestyle trends. Retailing is undergoing many changes as a result of changing consumer demand.

(*a*) Shopping is now to a large extent part of consumers' leisure activity. Previously, shopping was essentially of the 'mission' type for essential goods such as foodstuffs, but now tends to be 'comparison' shopping for clothing, furniture, and luxury items seen to be important as part of one's lifestyle. Retailers have therefore to cater for this development by providing amenities such as car-parking and eating facilities to ensure the comfort of shoppers.

(*b*) As shopping has become largely a leisure activity, so has the demand for longer opening hours increased. Late-night shopping on selected evenings of the week is now a normal feature in most shopping centres, and Sunday opening for many types of shop is now accepted.

(*c*) Consumer demand in recent years has been for shops such as Tie Rack and Sock Shop, which specialize in one type of product. Part of the reason for the appeal of these speciality shops is the consumer's quest for exclusiveness in place of previous acceptance of mass produced items, also shown in the popularity of natural materials such as wool over artifical fabrics.

(*d*) Shops have been more conscious in recent times of the need to establish an image in order to ensure attracting a specific sector of the market. The success of stores such as Next and Principles, for example, is based upon the appeal to 25 to 40 year olds in the professional sector, and store design and layout, as well as the products, emphasize this image.

16. Methods of payment. Rapid developments have also been made in the means of paying for goods and services purchased.

(*a*) *Credit cards* are used increasingly by purchasers, and especially 'in-store' cards issued by stores such as Hepworth's for their customers.

(*b*) Technological developments enable payments to be made faster, for example, through the EFT/POS system (*electronic funds transfer at point of sale*) which provides a detailed receipt for customers and enables stock records and other information to be kept by the store.

Wholesaling

17. Introduction. Traditionally, the wholesaler provides the link between the producers of the goods and services and the distributors who supply them to the public. With the increase of large-scale business there has been a tendency to eliminate the wholesaler; manufacturers seek to cut costs by selling direct to the public, and large multiple retail chains buy in bulk directly from manufacturers.

18. Functions of the wholesaler. Although many traditional wholesale firms have gone out of business, the important functions of wholesaling remain:

(*a*) 'breaking bulk' by receiving goods in large quantities and making them available to retailers in smaller quantities. Sometimes services such as packing and blending of products such as tea and coffee may be provided;

(*b*) goods are stored at warehouses until needed, at which retailers are able to view a wide range of products;

(*c*) trade credit may be available to retailers allowing payment for goods at a later date;

(*d*) delivery of goods may be provided, but many warehouses now offer a 'cash and carry' service whereby goods can be selected in small quantities and taken away more cheaply;

(*e*) the wholesaler may be an important source for both supplier and retailers of advice on market trends.

19. Commodity markets. Many commodities are traditionally supplied wholesale via specialist wholesalers and commodity markets. Many towns have specialized wholesalers for products such as meat, vegetables, fruit, and fish, while London has a number of commodity markets and exchanges. Britain's importance in international trade in the past meant that many products were brought to London for distribution to other parts of the world, and the tradition continues today.

(*a*) Wholesale commodity markets such as London Central Markets (Smithfield) and New Covent Garden are centrally located for retailers to buy and collect produce. Smithfield, where 3,000 people are employed on a site covering over 10 acres, specializes in the distribution of meat and poultry. Deliveries of meat, from abattoirs throughout Britain and from overseas, are received during the night, and the market starts trading from 5 am. Retailers examine produce and make their purchases directly from 80 wholesalers' stalls, transport usually being effected immediately upon purchase. Prices vary over the course of the morning's trading, and the price level at Smithfield has effects upon meat prices in Britain and other countries. New Covent Garden provides a similar service for fruit and vegetables.

(*b*) Most of the London commodity markets act as exchanges for commodities by providing for examination of samples or description of products. The London Corn Exchange dates back to the 18th century and reflects the importance of Britain in international trade in corn in that century. The London Commodity Exchange deals with products such as rubber, coffee, and sugar, while the London Metal Exchange organizes the sale of tin, copper and other important metals. The form of procedure differs between markets: tea and tobacco are sold by auction, representatives for large firms bidding for large quantities on the basis of samples supplied; other commodities, such as wheat and cotton are sold by private treaty, based upon a grading system for the commodity. Some markets provide a 'spot' market where a price is agreed and payment and delivery made immediately. Many markets, however, such as the metals market, operate as 'futures' markets whereby purchase is made for delivery at a future time, thus ensuring that future supplies of the commodity are guaranteed and that prices remain reasonably stable.

Case 9 Tesco's distribution system

Tesco – Britain's biggest retailer – obtained its supplies in the traditional way from a large number of manufacturers, who normally delivered direct to stores. Recently, however, Tesco introduced a centralized distribution system whereby buying and distribution is organized centrally at the firm's headquarters at Cheshunt in Hertfordshire.

All 380 Tesco stores have a direct computer link with Stock Control at head office, and details of their stock of various items is phoned to Cheshunt by each branch. Each store's needs and the timing of deliveries is then accomplished by computer, based upon this information. Deliveries are made by day and night from Tesco's seven main regional depots, by a large fleet of vehicles directly to stores. More regional depots are to be set up, as 'composite' depots providing for storage of almost all products, including frozen foods, and these are to be operated by a third party distributor, and not by Tesco.

Tesco superstores have warehouses included as part of the building, and 24 hour operation means that night staff are able to receive deliveries and stock shelves. The efficiency of the centralized distribution system is vital to the operation of the firm and means that stores are able to keep lower stocks and thus have more of their space for sales rather than storage.

Progress test 9

1. What is distribution? (**1**)
2. What are the functions of retailers? (**4**)
3. List the main types of retailing. (**5**)
4. Explain the continuing popularity of small shops. (**6**)
5. What is the importance of multiples today? (**8**)
6. Describe how mail order selling is organized. (**10**)
7. What do you understand by direct selling? (**11**)
8. Discuss the main current retailing trends. (**13–16**)
9. What is the function of wholesaling? (**17**)
10. Describe the importance of commodity markets. (**19**)
11. Describe how Tesco's centralized distribution system works. (**Case 9**)
12. What advantages does improved distribution bring to the firm? (**Case 9**)

10

Transport and communications

The importance of transport

1. The role of transport. Business depends heavily upon physical distribution – the actual movement of goods from producer to consumer. Its importance in today's world is shown by the increasing level of investment in newer and more sophisticated modes of transport, and it is estimated that as much as 25 per cent of the purchase price of a product is accounted for by distribution costs.

2. The functions of transport. Transport services provide a number of vital functions.

(*a*) Links the various stages of the production process, and promotes greater specialization;
(*b*) Provides services to people as workers and consumers;
(*c*) Provides for movement of goods and raw materials and reduces stock-holding;
(*d*) Aids the development of international trade.

3. The choice of transport. Careful consideration has to be given to the following factors in deciding what type of transport will be chosen:

(*a*) cost;
(*b*) speed and urgency of delivery;
(*c*) nature, size, weight, and bulk of the goods;
(*d*) length of journey;

(*e*) value of product;
(*f*) convenience of collection and delivery.

Forms of transport

4. Six main forms. The main forms of transport are:

(*a*) road;
(*b*) rail;
(*c*) air;
(*d*) inland waterways;
(*e*) sea;
(*f*) pipeline.

5. Road. Road transport has become the most significant form of transport both for business and general use. In Britain, over 80 per cent of freight moved within the country is carried by road, and the volume is increasing every year. Central Government is responsible for the building and maintenance of trunk roads in Britain while county councils are responsible for minor roads. Major roads and motorways provide a network linking main centres of population and industrial areas, and carry a large proportion of heavy traffic. Since the construction of the first motorway, the M1 in 1959, the system has been continually expanded, and a major landmark was the completion of the M25 London orbital route.

Carriage of passengers and freight is provided by privately-owned firms. About two-thirds of freight carried within Britain travels by vehicles owned by producers, retailers, or wholesalers, and the rest is transported by 'common carriers'. These are mostly small haulage firms, but the market is dominated by the National Freight Consortium which was formerly Government owned, and includes such well-known names as Pickfords and BRS (British Road Services).

The benefits of road transport are that it:

(*a*) provides a direct door-to-door service;
(*b*) involves less handling than other forms of transport and therefore there is less chance of loss or damage;
(*c*) is quick, especially over short distances;

(*d*) offers freedom of choice of routes and timing;

(*e*) is sometimes the only form of transport possible for remote areas;

(*f*) can often be used to supplement other forms of transport;

(*g*) can be tailored to needs of firms and their supply depots.

The drawbacks are:

(*a*) road transport is expensive for bulky commodities and long distances;

(*b*) congestion often increases time of journey;

(*c*) environmental effects such as pollution, noise, and congestion;

(*d*) high accident rates

(*e*) many roads are unsuitable for increasingly large lorries.

6. Rail transport. Railways were a vital aspect of the industrial development of most economies, but during this century many cutbacks have been made as other forms of transport have become more economic. In Britain, railways are under public ownership (since the Transport Act, 1947), and are the responsibility of British Rail.

In recent years, the country's extensive rail network has been considerably reduced in order to improve services by concentrating resources upon main inter-city routes. Passengers have been encouraged to use rail travel by bargain offers, for example,saver tickets to main cities, and modernization of freight services has taken place in order to make rail transport more cost-effective. British Rail recognizes the need to establish an image for itself as a market-led, consumer-orientated business with modern facilities, improved customer relations, and improved rolling stock, such as the high speed train. High speed freight services between major industrial centres depends upon better-equipped terminals and a computer-based total operations processing system.

The advantages of rail transport include the following:

(*a*) speed, especially over long distances;

(*b*) it is reasonably cheap for long-distance travel;

(*c*) purpose-built wagons for bulky goods such as oil, coal, and cement are available;

(*d*) it is economical in the use of fuel and labour;

(*e*) large firms can have their own sidings and warehouses;
(*f*) company trains can be operated for one customer.

The disadvantages are that:

(a) it is costly for short distance travel;
(*b*) it depends upon another form of transport, such as road for inland links;
(*c*) occasional delays are possible.

Railway systems offer a more efficient form of travel for urban use as congestion upon roads can be considerably reduced. Many cities, such as New York and Paris, have their own underground systems, while the Tokyo Monorail may be an indication of potential future development. In Britain, a light rapid transit system has been in use on Tyneside for some years, and the Docklands Light Railway in London, using automatically-operated trains, provides an important rail link.

7. Air. The increasing demand for rapid transit of people and freight has resulted in many recent developments in air travel. Developments of faster and more sophisticated aircraft such as Concorde provide important international links for people, while the air-freight industry is expanding with the use of wide-bodied cargo aircraft with bigger capacities. The holiday industry is dominated by the use of air travel for package holidays, while there is a rapidly expanding international courier market for the speedy delivery of small parcels.

Most countries have one leading airline, frequently state-owned. In Britain, the previously state-owned British Airways was privatized in 1987 and a merger proposed with privately-owned British Caledonian. All airports in Britain, such as the London airports of Heathrow and Gatwick and the provincial airports at Manchester and Birmingham, have been considerably extended in recent years to accommodate increasing traffic. Internal routes are being developed, like the 'shuttle' services between airports, and another important development is the 'STOL' (Short Take-Off and Landing) aircraft to serve urban areas, e.g. the London Docklands Airport.

The advantages of air transport are:

(*a*) it is the fastest form of distance travel for passengers;
(*b*) it is suitable for freight which is light and high-value;
(*c*) it is useful for commodities required urgently;
(*d*) shorter journey times for freight may reduce costs such as insurance.

The disadvantages are:

(*a*) high costs for many goods which may be heavy, large, or bulky;
(*b*) high operating costs of aircraft and airports;
(*c*) a supplementary form of transport is needed to link with airports;
(*d*) environmental objections, especially to noise, in airport vicinities.

8. Sea. Three-quarters of the earth's surface is water and therefore sea-borne transport of passengers and goods has always been important, especially with the development of international trade. Recent times have seen a decline in sea transport, however, as pressures of time have forced the use of other means such as air travel, and world shipping has suffered from over-capacity for a number of years.

Most shipping today is purpose-built for the cargoes it carries, such as oil-tankers, container ships, liners, roll-on/roll-off ferries, and bulk-ore carriers. An important international market for chartering ships is the Baltic Exchange in London, at which ships can be hired for a voyage or for a specific length of time.

Efficient port facilities are obviously essential to sea-borne transport. Ideal port requirements are deep-water access, modern handling equipment, maintenance facilities, good communications, Customs services, and a good labour record.

The advantages of sea transport include:

(*a*) easy access to most destinations and flexibility of route;
(*b*) especially suitable for transport of heavy materials;
(*c*) economies of scale by development of large ships and supertankers.

The disadvantages are:

(*a*) sea transport is relatively slow compared to other forms of transport;
(*b*) delays because of weather conditions;
(*c*) bad image of many docks, for example, high port charges and labour trouble.

9. Inland waterways. Transport by rivers and artificially created waterways (canals) served a vital function in the carriage of many commodities in the early years of Britain's industrial development. Today, however, the volume carried is small compared to that moved by other forms of transport. About half of Britain's inland waterways are in state-ownership (British Waterways Board) and they have been classified into Commercial Waterways for the carriage of freight, and Cruising Waterways to cater for leisure pursuits. Attempts have been made at improvements by such facilities as automatic locks and bridges, and more sophisticated barge-carrying systems such as BACAT, LASH, and SEABEE.

The benefits of inland waterway transport are:

(*a*) it is relatively cheap for heavy and bulky goods, e.g. coal, oil, gravel;
(*b*) it is cost-effective in terms of fuel use;
(*c*) it provides recreational facilities, drainage, and water supply.

The main drawback is that inland waterway transport is extremely slow.

10. Containerization. The most significant trend in freight transport in recent years has been containerization, by which goods previously carried and handled separately are packed in a closed container and carried as one item to the destination. Containerization now dominates most modes of transport, and many forms are interchangeable, for example, between road and rail. Air transport, however, requires specially constructed 'igloo' containers for new, wide-bodied aircraft, while purpose-built 'cellular' ships to take containers are increasing in number.

The advantages of containerization are:

(*a*) it offers a 'door-to-door' service;

(*b*) goods are not handled once packed;
(*c*) lower handling charges;
(*d*) less chance of loss, theft, or damage;
(*e*) improved handling systems shorten journey times;
(*f*) greater flexibility in the dispatch of goods.

The main disadvantage is the high cost of containers and handling equipment.

11. Pipeline. For materials such as gas and oil, the most effective form of delivery has been found to be by pipeline.

Communications

12. Definition. Communication is the passing of information or the indication of an opinion or decision in such a way that it is received and understood. It can be accomplished in a variety of ways and developments in technology are ensuring continually more rapid and effective means of communication. At a simple level, communication can be achieved by personal contact by the spoken word. Written messages sent by a postal system are a traditional form of communication, while devlopments in telecommunications have made the telephone and associated equipment vital in all walks of life today. Communication is also the function of 'the media' – the collective name for the press, radio, and television upon which we depend for information and entertainment.

13. Communications and business. The demanding nature of business today makes rapid contact between people and organizations essential. Early development of the means of communication can be said to have followed industrial and commercial expansion – at the beginning of the Industrial Revolution communication could only be made by messages carried by hand but by the end of the 19th century letters, telegrams, and the telephone had been introduced. Today business in general is dominated by high technology as trading becomes international – international money markets are highly dependent upon instant transmission of information immediately by computers and satellite links.

Postal communications

14. Postal services in Britain. The Post Office is one of the world's largest postal services organizations and has a monopoly on the carriage of letters. Some elements of competition have been introduced in recent years, for example the handling of parcels costing over £1 and the transfer of mail betweeen document exchanges have brought a number of private firms such as TNT into competition with the Post Office.

15. Development of the Post Office. Postal communication in Britain was pioneered by the Post Office. Originally it was a government department which came into being over 350 years ago when the king allowed private correspondence to be carried with the 'Royal Mail' – a title still used today. The introduction of the Penny Post in 1840 provided a cheap nationwide service by imposing a low flat-rate charge (pre-paid by adhesive stamps) and paved the way towards the development of the Post Office as one of the world's largest postal services.

16. Organization of the Post Office. In 1969 the Post Office ceased to be a government department and became a public corporation. Its powers and responsbilities are defined by government and it has a statutory obligation to collect and deliver mail throughout the country, and to arrange its finances within government guidelines and directions. As with all nationalized industries it has to ensure that the needs of the consumer are being met, and the Post Office Users' National Council is a statutory body set up for this purpose. The Mail Users' Association, an independent body formed by big business mail users, also acts as a watchdog over postal services. In 1981 the Post Office was separated from its telecommunications operations with the establishment of British Telecom (*see* 22 below). Re-structuring of services is taking place by the creation of specialist divisions, such as Girobank plc, and Post Office Counters plc, which are now both public limited companies, wholly-owned by the Post Office.

17. Structure of the Post Office. The Post Office provides four separate but inter-dependent businesses, involving important aspects of banking, retailing, and transport.

(*a*) Royal Mail Letters, responsible for collection and delivery of letters and packets throughout the U.K. and overseas.

(*b*) Royal Mail Parcels, which handles parcel deliveries, especially for business.

(*c*) Post Office Counters plc, a separate division which manages the business of the 22,000 post offices.

(*d*) Girobank plc, the Post Office's banking division whose services are available at post offices.

18. The Royal Mail. The Royal Mail collects and delivers a wide variety of mail, including letters and parcels. An extensive network of transport arrangements exists, using road, rail, and air – the familiar Royal Mail vans on the roads; British Rail services including Travelling Post Offices; and the increasing use of air transport for overnight delivery of mail to remote parts of the country.

(*a*) *Letter post* provides a valuable service to business, and almost half of all inland letter mail can be described as financial, consisting of bills, invoices, receipts, and orders. The service is divided into first-class and second-class, and the completion of the network of automated sorting offices using post-codes is improving next-day delivery of first-class mail. Among the most important facilities for business users of letter mail are *freepost*, by which a firm can pay an annual fee for a freepost address to which people can then write without attaching a stamp: *registered post* which provides compensation for loss: *recorded delivery* for important documents; and the *business reply service* whereby customers can return mail already stamped by a firm. In recent years there has been a considerable growth of direct mail as business has found that sending advertising directly to selected customers is a valuable marketing strategy.

(*b*) *Parcel post* services are organized upon a nationwide network of road, rail, and air delivery. This is a sector in which the Post Office has suffered in competition with private carriers, but improvements are being effected in order to attract business clients.

19. Post Office Counters. There are 22,000 post offices in the

United Kingdom, 1,600 of which are Crown Post Offices staffed by post office employees. The rest are sub-post offices run on an agency basis, usually as part of a privately-owned general store. They are all under the overall management of Post Office Counters plc and provide a wide range of services as part of the largest chain of retail outlets in the country:

(*a*) handling Royal Mail letters and parcels;
(*b*) girobank facilities are available at most post offices;
(*c*) retailing postage stamps and other items;
(*d*) agency services for Government departments, such as:
(*i*) motor vehicle licences for the Department of Transport;
(*ii*) benefits and pensions for the Department of Health and Social Security;
(*iii*) passports for the Foreign and Commonwealth Office;
(*iv*) TV licences for the Home Office.
(*e*) agency services for other bodies, such as:
(*i*) receiving telephone accounts for British Telecom;
(*ii*) railcards for senior citizens and families for British Rail;
(*iii*) sale of home help stamps for local councils;
(*iv*) cash dispensing facilities for building societies and other financial institutions via the LINK organization.

20. Specialist services. The Post Office offers a range of specialist services.

(*a*) *Datapost* is an overnight, door-to-door service which guarantees next-day delivery anywhere within the UK. It is a fast and reliable business service, using road, rail, and air transport to carry business documents and papers as well as parcels requiring urgent attention, such as spare parts, machine tools, or blood samples. Datapost International uses scheduled airline services to extend the service to other world business centres.

(*b*) *Intelpost* is a high-speed electronic facsimile transmission service by which documents handed in at a post office can be transmitted electronically throughout much of the country and to a number of other countries. Introduced in 1980, it was the world's first public facsimile transmission service.

(*c*) *Electronic post* is a computer based laser printing service which allows material such as graphs, logos, and signatures, as well as text, to be processed and mailed for next-day delivery.

Telecommunications

21. Introduction. The telecommunications industry is one of the world's fastest growing industries, based upon continually developing technology. It is a vital aspect of business today as information and decisions can be obtained instantly, often on a worldwide basis by the extensive use of communications satellites. A wide variety of telecommunications systems and equipment exist, including developments of the telephone, such as computer links and car phones, teleprinter systems like Teletex, and television based systems such as Prestel.

22. Structure of the British telecommunications industry. Telecommunications was initially part of the Post Office until the British Telecommunications Act 1981 divided postal services (which remained with the Post Office), and telecommunications, which became the responsibility of another public corporation – British Telecom – with a statutory monopoly in telecommunications. By the Telecommunications Act 1984 British Telecom became a public limited company with a majority of voting shares sold to private investors.

(*a*) The 1984 Act also removed British Telecom's statutory monopoly by enabling other bodies to be licensed to provide certain services. British Telecom has the obligation of having to ensure the existence of a telecommunications system throughout the country and to provide certain basic services such as emergency services and public call box facilities.

(*b*) Another company – Mercury Communications Ltd – has been licensed as the second major provider of telecommunications services. It offers a wide range of services, nationally and internationally, and is establishing a new telephone network based in Birmingham, intended to attract the business market.

(*c*) By the licensing arrangements set down in 1982 to foster competition in the industry; private firms can supply, install, and maintain most types of equipment.

(*d*) The Office of Telecommunications (OFTEL) was established by the 1984 Act to be the regulatory body for the telecommunications industry. Its role is to ensure that companies obtaining licences comply with the required conditions; to promote competition in the industry; and to act on behalf of consumers by investigating complaints.

23. Telephone services. An effective telephone system is essential for business. Because of the increasing demands placed upon it, improvements are constantly necessary, and the major recent development has been British Telecom's *System X* – a national digital computerized network. The new system should increase efficiency by speeding up connections and by flexibility in finding unengaged lines. A wide range of telephone services are available, such as :

(*a*) *freefone*, by which a firm, upon payment of a fee, can allow customers to make calls via the operator without charge to the customer. The automatic *linkline* service allows contact to be made anywhere in the country,
(*b*) information services such as *timeline* (speaking clock);
(*c*) *phonecard services* providing for prepaid calls to be made;
(*d*) *cellular radio* facilities for cars and other vehicles;
(*e*) *radiopaging* services providing signals for urgent messages.

24. Other services. New services, both for private and business use, are becoming available, such as:

(*a*) *viewdata* services which, by telephone connection to television, make information available upon the screen. British Telecom's Prestel service, introduced in 1979, now offers a wide range of information and can be linked to other databases providing, e.g. home shopping and banking facilities.
(*b*) *teletext* systems such as Ceefax and Oracle provide data transmission via the BBC (Ceefax) and ITV (Oracle) of a wide range of information and current events.
(*c*) *Confravision*, which enables conferences to be held between businessmen separated by long distances. In addition to making interactive discussion between a number of people possible, it has

the advantage of making the people visible and also enables information to be transmitted simultaneously.

Case 10 Electronic mail by Telecom Gold

The pace of business life today makes rapid forms of communication between people and organizations vital. The conventional methods of postal services and telephone have served business and industry well for very many years, but the linking of computer technology with telecommunications now make electronic mail (or '*email*') an exciting development at the present time. Electronic mail is simply a means of sending written messages from one computer to another, using the public telephone service.

Telecom Gold is the main electronic mail service offered by British Telecommunications plc. It was set up in 1981, based upon the USA Dialcom electronic mail service, and now has over 105,000 subscribers. It is an open system in which most types of microcomputer or word processor can be used, and the service caters for a wide variety of business and private uses. John Menzies, one of the largest suppliers of books to libraries worldwide, uses Telecom Gold to update customers' lists weekly, it is used by Tesco for transmitting orders to suppliers, while firms in general find it an effective means of circulating information to depots and branches.

To use Telecom Gold, a subscriber first connects to TG via the telephone network by means of a modem and suitable communications software. A message can then be typed out on the keyboard, which is converted by a modem into signals which are sent down the telephone line to the Telecom Gold computer. By means of a mailbox number given to every subscriber, the message is then sent to the terminal of the recipient where it appears on the screen.

Telecom Gold offers a number of important advantages. It is a fast, reliable, simple, and convenient means of communication, and is also inexpensive. If written messages are needed it can be linked to telex, and it has the important advantage that it is part of an expanding international electronic mail system.

Progress test 10

1. What are the functions of transport? (**2**)
2. How are choices made between forms of transport? (**3**)
3. What are the advantages of the following forms of transport? (*a*) Road (**5**), (*b*) Rail (**6**), (*c*) Air (**7**), (*d*) Sea (**8**).
4. What improvements have been made in inland waterways? (**9**)
5. What is containerization? What are its advantages? (**10**)
6. What do you understand by *communications*? (**12**)
7. Describe the role of the Post Office. How is it organized? (**15,16**)
8. What types of business activities does the Post Office provide? (**17**)
9. Describe the main Royal Mail services. (**18**)
10. What services may be available at the Post Office? (**19**)
11. Describe the organization of telecommunications in Britain. (**22**)
12. How important is the telephone to business? (**23**)
13. What are the following services? (*a*) Viewdata, (*b*) Teletext, (*c*) Confravision. (**24**)
14. What is electronic mail? (**Case 10**)
15. What advantages does Telecom Gold offer business? (**Case 10**)

11

Banking and finance

Money

1. Introduction. The finance of business depends upon money and the banking system. Money has been described as the life-blood of a modern economy, and a country's economic well-being is usually judged by the value of its currency on the foreign exchange markets.

2. Functions. Money serves a number of vital functions:

(*a*) a medium of exchange;
(*b*) a measure of value;
(*c*) a store of value;
(*d*) a standard for deferred payments.

Money enables business to take place by making goods and services available to those in need of them. Today we accept money – in all the various currencies and denominations of the world – as the commodity which allows these transactions to take place.

3. Barter. Before money came into existence, barter, i.e. the direct exchange of goods between people, was the only means by which a variety of goods could be made available. The problems involved in finding people and commodities which could be directly exchanged, however, made barter exceptionally difficult, and thus commodities such as precious metals (or even rare cowrie shells) came to serve as money. Barter is still used occasionally today whenever monetary difficulties occur (e.g. in obtaining acceptable exchange of foreign currencies) when countries may agree upon an exchange of products by 'counter-trade'.(See **Case 11**.)

4. Qualities. In order that a commodity should serve as an effective coinage, several qualities are necessary. It should be:

(*a*) acceptable to everyone;
(*b*) long-lasting;
(*c*) scarce;
(*d*) divisible;
(*e*) portable.

5. Money supply. The kinds of money in use are as follows:

(*a*) *Coins and notes*. Coins, such as the sovereign, were once made of precious metals such as gold, but today are usually made of bronze or alloys of copper and nickel. In Britain, coins are produced at the Royal Mint, and, with bank notes in various denominations issued by the Bank of England are legal tender, i.e. they must be accepted in law for settlement of transactions.

(*b*) *Bank deposits*. Bank deposits act as money because a large proportion of debts (in Britain, about 80 per cent in value of all transactions) are paid for by cheque, i.e. a transfer of money from one person's bank account to that of another. Bank deposits may be 'sight' deposits kept in current accounts or 'time' deposits in deposit accounts, but in today's competitive banking world a wide range of various forms of account exist.

Attempts are made to measure the money supply, but it is obviously a difficult task bearing in mind the many different forms of bank account and banking institution. In Britain several measures of the money supply have been attempted, such as *M0* (mainly notes and coins in circulation) which is the 'narrow' measure of money, indicating immediate purchasing power; and *M3* (a wide range of bank deposits which require notice of withdrawal) and which is thus the 'broad' measure of the money supply, indicating the potential purchasing power in the economy which could result if those bank deposits were turned into cash.

Banking

6. Banking and business. A nation's business life depends heavily upon its banking system. Banking serves the business community in a number of ways by arranging means of payment between producer and consumer and by producing capital for business from the many deposits it receives. The banking system consists of three elements – central banking, commercial banking, and a range of other institutions such as merchant banks which arrange loans for business.

7. Central banking. The importance of the banking and financial system of a country is such that a government will seek to maintain some form of control over it. It is important, for example, that the money supply is adequate to the needs of business and that the value of the nation's currency is maintained. Therefore a country's central bank occupies an important supervisory role. In the USA this function is fulfilled by the Federal Reserve System and in France by the Bank of France.

8. Bank of England. In Britain, the central bank is the Bank of England, established in 1694. It gradually achieved a position of prominence over the banking system and it was nationalized in 1946. Its Governor and directors are appointed by the Crown on the recommendation of the Prime Minister.

The main functions and responsibilities of the Bank of England are:

(*a*) to supervize the banking system by carrying out the government's monetary policy and by taking action as necessary to correct faults;

(*b*) to act as the government's bank by keeping state accounts, including the National Debt, and by advising the government on financial matters;

(*c*) to serve as banker to the rest of the banking system by keeping deposits of other banks;

(*d*) to be responsible for the issue of bank notes in the UK (Scotland and Northern Ireland also arrange a small note issue).

(*e*) to keep gold reserves (in the Exchange Equalization Account) and to arrange settlement of overseas debt;

(*f*) to act as the 'lender of last resort' by ensuring that the commercial banks are able to recall deposits;

(*g*) to liaise with the central banks of other countries and with international bodies such as the IMF (International Monetary Fund).

Commercial banking

9. Definition. For the general public as well as for the business community, the most important part of the banking system is the commercial banking sector. In Britain, this is represented by the 'Big Four' banks – National Westminster, Lloyds, Midland, and Barclays – who have a network of branches throughout the country. They are sometimes referred to as the *clearing banks* as they are members of the Bankers' Clearing House which organizes the settlement of debts between them.

10. The functions of commercial banking.

(*a*) To accept deposits of money and valuables for safe keeping.
(*b*) To provide loans and finance to business and individuals.
(*c*) To arrange and make payments on behalf of customers.
(*d*) To provide a wide range of services, e.g. trusteeship.

11. Services of the commercial banks. Banking is a fiercely competitive industry and all banks provide a range of services for their customers, including:

(*a*) making payments in a variety of ways (*see* **15** below);

(*b*) providing loans to customers, e.g. house mortgages, personal loans;

(*c*) placing money, valuables, and documents in safe keeping;

(*d*) providing 'out-of-hours' services, e.g. cash dispensers, night safes;

(*e*) arranging foreign exchange transactions, e.g. foreign currency;

(*f*) advice on matters such as taxation, company finance;

(*g*) purchase and sale of stocks and shares;

(*h*) acting as executors and trustees of wills;

(*i*) providing references for customers, e.g. for accounts at shops.

12. Bank accounts. Customers choose the types of account which best suit their banking needs. Traditionally, accounts are *current accounts* for eveyday use and *deposit accounts* in which money is probably left for some time. However, competition between banks and other financial institutions in recent years has seen other types of account offered to customers.

(*a*) *Current accounts.* Money for day-to-day use is normally kept in a current account. People and businesses draw upon these accounts for normal everyday living expenses and for making transactions, usually by cheque (*see* **17** below) or by cash dispenser. Banks make charges to customers for payments made from current accounts, but in the more competitive environment of recent years many have offered 'free banking' or even interest to customers who maintain a certain level of deposit in their current account. Customers who, on the other hand, may need more finance temporarily, may be provided with *overdraft* facilities on their account, entitling them to write a cheque in excess of the money in their account. A statement of account is sent to customers at intervals or can be requested at any time. References usually have to be provided to the bank before an account can be opened, and various arrangements can be made, e.g. a married couple may have a joint account or a club or business may have an account which would allow a number of signatories to sign cheques on its behalf.

(*b*) *Deposit accounts.* A deposit account is normally opened by a private individual as a saving account. Deposits into the account are made by credit slips and interest is paid by the bank. A certain period of time (usually seven days) is required by the bank for payments to be made from the deposit account, and a cheque book is not provided. Statements of account are provided as with current accounts but overdraft facilities are not given.

(*c*) *Budget accounts.* To cater for regular payments, such as gas and electricity bills, budget accounts have been introduced by banks. Customers make deposits into the account at regular intervals (usually monthly), and bills can then be met from the account whenever they fall due. The anticipated payments for a year will be calculated by the customer who informs the bank of the likely amounts and the dates due. Cheques can then be written to cover the bills due and at the end of a year the account should balance, the amount paid in bills equal to the regular deposits paid in by the account holder. The account has the advantage of ensuring that bills can be met at any stage during the year, even though a few heavy bills may fall due at the same time. It is therefore a considerable help to budgeting. A service charge is made by the bank to cover the cost of making payments.

(*d*) *Loan accounts*. Consumer demand for credit in recent years has led to the development of new forms of bank lending by accounts which may be opened by a customer specifically for loan facilities. A variation on this form of account is the *save-and-borrow* account into which regular payments are made by the account holder who can then opt either to receive interest on the money as it accrues in the account or to use the credit available.

13. Assets and liabilities. Banks must be able to balance their books by ensuring that their liabilities, i.e. the amounts owed to customers, are covered by assets, i.e. the amount in the bank's possession or the amounts owed by other customers. Banks have two main aims – *profitability* and *liquidity* – and while on one hand a bank has to be able to satisfy its customers' demand for cash withdrawals, it also has to satisfy its shareholders' interest in profitability. The bank will therefore try to meet these two demands by arranging its assets in order to provide both liquidity *and* profitability. Its most liquid asset – cash – will be the least profitable, while the loans its makes to customers are the most profitable but the least liquid, earning the bank a high rate of interest but being repaid over a relatively long period of time, and with some risk of default.

14. Creation of credit. Banks have found by experience that only a small proportion of the money deposited with them is required for immediate withdrawals of cash by customers. Every deposit made therefore allows the bank to use the money to advance loans to other customers, keeping only part of it to meet any demand for repayment. Thus, with every new deposit the bank is able to provide other customers with loans – a highly profitable area.

It is essential, however, that banks do not create too great an amount of credit as they could find themselves with insufficient cash to meet demands for withdrawals by customers. In the past, bankers have had an agreed amount of money kept as cash – about 8 per cent of the deposits – but in recent times the Bank of England has maintained strict control over this ratio. Although the Bank of England supervises the banks informally – requiring 'prudential standards of liquidity' – banks have to keep a cash ratio with the Bank of England as well as having to ensure that some of their assets are liquid.

15. Making payments. Payment for goods and services received can be made in a number of ways and via various institutions. Despite the many disadvantages, payment in cash remains popular in Britain, and in other countries also the use of cash in the 'black economy' is popular.

16. Bank methods of payment.

(*a*) *Cheques* (*see* **18**) are still the most popular means of payment.

(*b*) *Bank giro.* Anyone can use bank facilities to make payments by bank giro, providing the person to be paid has a bank account. Payment is made by the bank's receipt of a sum of money which is then simply transferred into the payee's bank account.

(*c*) *Credit transfer* provides for the settlement of bills by, as the name suggests, the transfer of credit from one bank account to another. Usually the debtor provides the bank with a list of creditors for regular payments, such as monthly salaries. The debtor then pays one cheque to the bank to cover all payments, and the individual sums are credited to the various accounts.

(*d*) *Direct debit.* Creditors are empowered by customers to obtain payment of a bill directly from a bank. This form of payment is becoming increasingly popular for payments to large organizations of regular bills which may vary somewhat in amount, such as gas and electricity accounts.

(*e*) *Standing orders* for payments of regular bills: customers instruct the bank to make payments, often from a special Budget Account (*see* **12**).

(*f*) *Banker's drafts* allow bank customer to make payments backed by the bank's authority. A banker's draft is, in effect, a cheque drawn by the bank on itself and is used where confirmation of credit-worthiness may be desirable, as, for example, in an overseas deal.

17. Cheques. A cheque is an instruction to a bank by one of its customers to transfer money from his or her account to the account of another person. All banks provide their customers with cheque books containing a number of cheques which can be drawn up by the *drawer* – the account-holder. Before it will be accepted by the bank it has to be correctly filled out with the date, the name of the person or organization to be paid (the *payee*), the sum of money expressed in numbers and words, and the drawer's signature which must match the specimen signature held by the bank. Details of the payment made are copied on to the counterfoil which remains in the chequebook as a reminder of how much has been paid out of the account.

Because of the popularity of cheques for making payments, care has to be taken to guard against fraud. Normally, a cheque is an 'open' cheque which can be made payable to anyone, but two lines across the face of the cheque make it a 'crossed' cheque which can only be paid into an account at a bank or building society. Crossed cheques are therefore a safer means of payment as the account into which they are paid can always be traced. A further safeguard against increasing fraud involving cheques was the introduction of the *cheque card*. These cards allow payments to be made to a firm by a person not known to them as a regular customer. Production of the card at the time of making out a cheque guarantees that the bank will pay the amount of the cheque up to the amount stated on the card, even if it cannot be covered by the customer's account. A cheque made out for an amount in excess of the sum in the account or beyond the account-holder's overdraft limit may be refused by the bank. It is said to have 'bounced' and the bank will inform the payee's bank that payment will not be made and return the cheque to the payee stamped 'refer to drawer'. The drawer will then have to arrange with the payee how payment is to be made, usually by asking the payee to re-present the cheque once adequate funds are ensured in the account to meet it. Occasionally a cheque may bounce because the account-holder has second thoughts over the payment made and decides to stop the cheque already presented by ordering the bank not to honour it.

Cheques have become a well-established means of payments for a number of reasons:

(*a*) A cheque is not money but an order to pay money and is therefore a safer method of payment than cash.

(*b*) For many regular payments such as wages and salaries, cheques are more efficient and safer than large cash withdrawals for distribution to employees.

(*c*) Cheques are legally accepted as proof of payment and receipts are not therefore necessary.

(*d*) Cheques are a simple and convenient way of making most payments.

18. Cheque clearing. Payments are made between people and organizations who are all customers of different banks, and the process by which bank accounts are debited and credited with the amounts on cheques is called *clearing*. Payment by a cheque is only complete once the cheque has been cleared. The institution which organizes the massive job of cheque clearing in Britain is the Bankers' Clearing House in London. The major commercial banks are all members of the Clearing House and are often referred to as *clearing banks*. Cheques are brought daily to the Clearing House and the amounts credited and debited to the member banks are totalled. Transfer of funds between the various banks is then made by details of the total amounts being passed to the Bank of England at which the banks have accounts. Adjustment between the banks' accounts are then made daily at the Bank of England.

In recent years the processing of cheques has become increasingly automated in order to simplify and speed up the operation. In 1969 the Bankers' Automated Clearing Service (BACS) was es tablished for regular transfers between clearing banks and a more recent innovation is the Clearing House Automated Payment System (CHAPS) for the electronic transfer of large sums the same day.

Post Office services

19. Post Office methods of payment. With the continuing increase in the number of people with bank accounts, the Post Office is used less for making payments than in the past.

(*a*) Stamps are frequently an easy way of paying very small amounts of money, especially when sent by post.

(*b*) When goods are sent by post, payment can often be made upon receipt by COD (cash on delivery).

(*c*) The postal order is a useful way of sending smaller sums of money by post. The maximum amount is £10 but specific amounts can be sent by using stamps.

(*d*) The giro system allows payments to be made by simple transfer of funds from one account to another.

Building societies

20. Definition. A major development in banking in Britain in recent years has been the growth of building societies. The building society is a unique financial institution which takes in deposits from individual savers and provides long-term loans for housing, based upon the security of the property.

21. Development. Originally established in the late 18th century to enable people to save and borrow for house purchase, building societies now provide a wide range of banking services.. Initially they were composed of groups of people who co-operated in buying land and building houses, and when everyone in the group was housed the society was then 'terminated'. They developed into 'permanent' societies (a name still found today) when they began to attract savings from depositors which were then lent to borrowers as *mortgages* for house purchase.

22. Organization. The basic legislative structure was the 1874 Building Societies Act and the societies operated under the jurisdiction of the Registrar of Friendly Societies. During the 1970s they began to compete for custom with banks and the Building Societies Act, 1986, conferred greater powers upon them to develop services and to become public limited companies if desired. Supervision of the societies is effected by the Building Societies Commission, to fulfil the role previously held by the Registrar of Friendly Societies. A building societies' Ombudsman was appointed in 1987 to investigate complaints by the public against societies.

23. Services. In addition to the provision of finance for house purchase by long-term loans against the security of property, most societies have now extended their range of services. A variety of savings schemes are available and more sophisticated payment systems including cheque and automated cash withdrawal facilities. Under the 1986 Act, societies can make unsecured loans to customers, and provide conveyancing and estate agency business for house purchase.

In a more competitive environment, the number of societies has declined, as larger societies have sought more market domination by merging, as was the case with Nationwide-Anglia.

Credit

24. Definition. By credit, goods and services may be obtained immediately and payment deferred until some future time or by regular payments. The advantages are such that both consumers and producers make use of various credit schemes. The main forms of credit are: hire purchase; credit sales; budget accounts; mail order; trade credit and credit cards.

25. Hire purchase. This is one of the most popular forms of credit by which – as the name suggests – goods may be held and used during the time that payments are being made, but only become the property of the purchaser upon payment of the final instalment. Goods are usually supplied upon payment of a deposit and, possibly, receipt of a reference. The debt is usually accepted by a specialist finance company, and full details of the transaction, including the cash price and responsibilities for repossession if payments lapse, are legally required. Hire purchase allows immediate use of the goods by the consumer, while the supplier can increase his or her business and obtain profit at once. However, purchase entails interest charges which have to be paid and there is a danger of overspending for the consumer.

26. Credit sales. Many large businesses prefer to offer credit sales agreements themselves than to offer hire purchase. The main difference is that the goods, once possessed, become the property of the customer. If the customer defaults in payments, the supplier cannot reclaim the goods and may have to resort to legal action, for payment.

27. Budget accounts. Many retail organizations provide budget accounts by which their customers pay regular fixed payments, usually weekly or monthly, and can then obtain goods up to a certain limit. It is a form of continuing credit, and has the advantage that new agreements are not required for each individual purchase.

28. Mail order. Mail order is a traditional form of credit (see Chapter 9) by which customers choose goods from a catalogue held by a local agent who arranges collection of payments on a weekly basis.

29. Trade credit. Many producers use credit to obtain materials and supplies of essential goods neccesary for business, which can then be paid for from continuing production.

30. Credit cards. As consumer demand for credit continued during the 1970s, credit cards were introduced and grew rapidly in popularity. The two main schemes – Barclaycard and Access – are organized by banks, and cards were issued to customers who were then able to use them at stores participating in the scheme. Customers – who have a set credit limit – obtain goods immediately and have to pay a set proportion of their total debt every month. Suppliers receive payment for the whole amount of the purchase price of the commodity from the credit card company. Credit cards have proved to be especially popular for making purchases by telephone, often as a result of TV advertisements.

31. Charge cards. American Express and Diners Club are two well-established examples of charge cards by which credit can be obtained as with credit cards. Unlike credit cards, however, a payment has to be made for them by cardholders, and settlement of the account has to be made on a monthly basis. In addition to the main credit cards, many stores have introduced their own 'in-store' or 'charge' cards which operate on the same principle.

Case 11 Bartering tractors for wine

Massey-Ferguson, the British tractor manufacturing firm, has an international market for its tractors. The company found that sales of its tractors were frequently frustrated by difficulties customers experienced in arranging the foreign exchange of currencies. To get around this problem Massey-Ferguson established its own Trade and Barter Division to promote other forms of international trade by arranging exchanges of products or counter trade.

In 1984 a number of Austrian wine growers were anxious to obtain Massey-Ferguson tractors for use in their vineyards. Massey-Ferguson was equally anxious to supply the tractors. Austria had been building up a 'wine lake' – a surplus which it was anxious to dispose of – for a number of years and Massey-Ferguson therefore negotiated a deal with its Austrian distributor, Austro-Diesel, whereby customers traded quantities of their wine in return for the tractors they needed. The deal depended upon the success of the firm's worldwide business contacts and distribution network in being able to find customers for the Austrian wine. The wine was later sold to British wine importers, so that Massey-Ferguson was eventually able to collect payment for its tractors.

Thus an important international deal had taken place by the old-fashioned method of barter. Difficulties in obtaining foreign exchange have been experienced by many countries, especially in the Eastern Bloc, and a willingness to use this form of counter-trade as in this example means that potential markets need not be lost.

Progress test 11

1. What are the functions of money? (**2**)
2. What is barter? What are its disadvantages? (**3**)

3. What qualities should money possess? (**4**)
4. What is the money supply? (**5**)
5. Describe the role of the Bank of England. (**8**)
6. What services do commercial banks offer? (**10**)
7. Explain the main types of bank account. (**12**)
8. How do banks create credit? (**13,14**)
9. What are the main means of making payments? (**15-19**)
10. What is a cheque? Explain its advantages for making payments. (**17**)
11. Describe the changing role of building societies. (**20-23**)
12. What are the main forms of credit? (**24-31**)
13. Explain how barter may help international trade. (**Case 11**)

12

Insurance

Introduction

1. Definition. Insurance is a means of dealing with the many risks which are met in business. It may be possible to avoid such risks in several ways, for example, by imposing stricter safety regulations, by following a more cautious trading policy, or by setting aside reserves to cover any losses which may occur. The combined sum set aside by a large national chain of retail stores, for instance, may be sufficient to offset the risk of damage to any one member of that chain – a form of self-insurance.

However, in today's vast and complicated business world it is far more likely that a business will safeguard against the many risks faced by obtaining insurance provided by specialist insurers.

2. Risks. Insurance is simply a means of dealing with *risk*. In return for a fee the insurer accepts the risk by undertaking to reimburse the insured if certain accidental occurrences should take place. But insurance can only be provided when the probability of loss can be calculated. It is based on the 'law of large numbers', by which predictions are made of how many fires, floods, deaths, or car crashes may occur in a given year. Predictions in insurance are based upon *actuarial tables* which are compiled from statistics of occurrences of misfortunes, for example, life expectancy can be calculated as a basis for life assurance.

However, accurate assessment is impossible for many business risks, such as a change in fashion, fall in demand, bad management, or international political problems. Such risks are therefore termed *uninsurable*.

3. How insurancc works. Insurance provides the means whereby protection from financial loss may be secured by 'pooling' or sharing risks with others. In return for a fee – or *premium* – an insurance company will accept a risk and provide compensation in the form of money if loss or damage should occur. The combined contribution of those who obtain insurance cover forms a fund out of which those who suffer loss or damage can be compensated, or *indemnified*. Thus, insurance enables the many who pay insurance premiums every year to gain peace of mind, while the unfortunate few who experience mishaps can, by reimbursement from the insurance company, be restored to the position they were in before their misfortune.

4. How insurance developed. It is natural for people to seek to minimize the many dangers and uncertainties of life, and so insurance in some form has always existed. Roman soldiers travelling to distant parts of the Roman Empire, early merchants and their fleets trading in uncharted waters, and medieval craftsmen fearing the loss of employment all made some provision for the dangers they faced. By 1601 the importance of insurance in Britain had been recognized in an Act of Parliament - 'By means of which policies of insurance...the loss lighteth rather more easily upon many than heavily upon few'. The Great Fire of London in 1666 saw the establishment of many insurance companies, while the prompt attention to claims arising from the San Francisco earthquake in 1906 gained British insurers an international reputation.

5. The role of insurance. Insurance performs four important functions in the modern business world.

(*a*) Protection is provided against financial loss.

(*b*) Enterprise is encouraged when firms eager to develop are provided with flexible and imaginative insurance protection.

(*c*) Premiums collected are invested in business and industry and provide funds for Government services.

(*d*) Wider share ownership is encouraged by investment of individual premiums.

6. The importance of insurance. As world trade has expanded, so too has the insurance industry grown. It is based mainly in Europe and North America and the needs of the rest of the world are served from these two areas.

The insurance industry is the UK's biggest source of foreign earnings, and in 1986 the overseas earnings of the UK insurance market was £4260 million. Over a third of British insurers' premium income is channelled back into business and industry as investment through the Stock Exchange, and a further fifth of those funds goes into Government stock to provide for such public sector services as hospitals, schools, and road-building. Employment in the insurance industry is growing, and in 1987 totalled 246,000.

Principles of insurance

7. Introduction. In order that the insurance industry is able to provide an effective service to business, four important principles have to be observed:

(*a*) insurable interest,
(*b*) utmost good faith,
(*c*) indemnity,
(*d*) proximate cause.

8. Insurable interest. An insurance contract can only be entered into if the person seeking insurance has a direct financial interest in the risk – an *insurable interest.* The risk could be damage to the person's premises, theft of stock, or ill-health, which would result in disruption to the business and financial loss. The principle therefore ensures that the insurance sought is a genuine safeguard against personal loss – the insured person would not be allowed to gamble on the possibility of similar mishaps affecting a business rival, for example.

9. Utmost good faith. It is a basic principle in law that a contract must be entered into in *utmost good faith* (*uberrimae fides*). The person seeking insurance therefore has to disclose all relevant details of the risk to be insured, while the insurance company similarly has to state clearly all the terms and conditions of the cover they are to provide. This principle is strictly applied, and even though a company's proposal form may not specify a certain aspect, the responsibility rests with the proposer to inform the insurer of any relevant factor, as the insurer has to rely upon the information provided in order to assess the risk. A contract entered into without this mutual understanding may become *void,* i.e. cease to exist.

Occasionally an insurance company will make an *ex gratia* payment, i.e. a sum less than the full compensation agreed in the contract, if facts material to the assessment of the risk have not been disclosed by the proposer.

10. Indemnity. Compensation received for a loss against which insurance cover had been obtained must restore a person to the position he or she was in before sustaining the misfortune. The principle of indemnity therefore is of considerable importance in insurance terms as the insurer undertakes to make good a client's loss, but not to allow the client to benefit by more than the extent of the loss, as that would mean that a profit was being made from the insurance cover. Reimbursement for a car, for example, would be calculated in terms of its age and condition so that the sum paid would be sufficient for the car to be replaced by one of approximately the same vintage – not a brand new car. There are two important aspects of indemnity – *contribution* and *subrogation.*

(*a*) *Contribution.* The scope and development of insurance in recent years makes it likely that some risks are covered by more than one policy, and possibly by more than one insurer. It would, of course, be contrary to the principle of indemnity to claim for the full amount of the loss from each of two insurers, and therefore, in practice, the claim would probably be met by the insurers involved deciding upon the proportions of the total reimbursement each would pay.

(*b*) *Subrogation.* By subrogation is meant the substitution of one person's rights by another, so that when a claim has been paid the insurer then inherits all the rights of the insured. For example, the owner of a car which has been 'written-off' by the insurers as a total wreck would receive the full value of the car as compensation. However, the wrecked vehicle still has a value in terms of its spare parts which the insurers, as the legal owners, can then sell.

11. Proximate cause. Before a claim can be allowed, it has to be firmly established that the exact cause of the mishap was,in fact, that which was insured against. An insurance policy will be quite specific about the nature of the risk undertaken and will possibly exclude certain risks. Insurers will therefore be anxious to establish the immediate – or *proximate* – cause. Confusion can arise, for example, over the exact cause of damage to goods in storage, which may be the direct result of fire,the result of smoke, or the result of using certain materials to combat the fire.

Types of insurance

12. Introduction. With rapid developments in business and industry, new risks are constantly presenting themselves. Most risks can be classified under four main headings – fire, life, accident, and marine.

13. Fire insurance. From the early days of fire insurance when companies operated their own fire brigades, fire-fighting has now become one of the public services. Insurers make stringent regulations about the provision of extinquishers, fire escapes, fire-doors, and possibly sprinkler systems if the possibility of damage is great. In addition to insuring against the direct results of fire, *consequential loss* – such as loss of business by the difficulty of replacing equipment – can also be covered.

14. Life assurance. There are three main types: *whole life*, *endowment*, and *term*. 'Assurance' is frequently used for life policies although it has become acceptable to use both 'insurance' and 'assurance'.

(*a*) *Whole life* is a form of policy in which payment is only made upon the death of the insured. A less popular form of insurance today, it is intended to provide for the insured's dependants in the event of death.

(*b*) *Endowment* is a more popular form of life insurance as it provides a form of saving in a variety of ways. Policies are normally payable at the end of a fixed term and can usually be surrendered, i.e. bonuses and part of the value can be recovered before the term of the cover is ended. Both Whole Life and Endowment policies can be with profits, i.e. the insured shares in the profits of the insurance company.

(*c*) *Term* insurance is a form of insurance in which the sum assured is only payable if death occurs within the agreed period of time. It is frequently used, for example, to provide low-cost cover for the period during which a house mortgage is being repaid, or by a firm to protect against the loss of a key executive.

15. Accident insurance. Industrialization brought with it a variety of new risks – the dangers of steam-powered machinery, the hazards of increasingly faster forms of transport, and the possibility of injury or ill-health which could deprive a worker of his or her livelihood. Accident insurance therefore today includes a wide range of risk. Among the more important types are: insurance of liability; fidelity guarantee; property insurance; bad debts; and motor insurance.

16. Insurance of liability. Insurance provides safeguards for those who have a responsibility to others. An employer, for example, is legally liable under the Employers' Liability (Compusory Insurance) Act, 1969 for injuries suffered by employees – particularly important if they are working in dangerous conditions or handling dangerous materials. Liability exists also to the customer, and insurance can provide cover against the risk of damage caused by goods sold or services provided, for example, food poisoning caused by the sale of contaminated foodstuffs.

17. Fidelity guarantee. Insurance cover can safeguard against financial loss as a result of theft or embezzlement by employees, for example, cashiers, who are in positions of trust.

18. Property insurance. Insurance against the high costs of business premises is essential, and can include, in addition to replacement, injuries caused or loss of business, for example, by breakage of a plate glass window.

19. Bad debts. Unpaid accounts are inevitable, and insurance cover can be provided to offset losses to some extent. The

Government provides an insurance service to exporters via the ECGD (Export Credits Guarantee Department) by reimburing firms for non-payment of goods exported.

20. Motor insurance. It is a legal requirement under the Road Traffic Act that every motorist has *third party* cover against personal injury suffered by another person as a result of the driver's negligence. Normally, insurance companies include this cover within policies which also include damage to other people's property. *Comprehensive* policies have become more popular as they provide the motorist with insurance against damage to his or her own vehicle. Premiums are calculated by reference to a range of criteria, including the age and accident record of the driver and the locality in which the vehicle is based. Motor insurance has become fiercely competitive in recent years as insurers have competed for business and costs of repairs continue to rise.

21. Marine insurance. This is one of the earliest forms of insurance and is of considerable importance today in terms of the size of present day ships and the value of cargoes. It also covers the danger of environmental pollution resulting from escape of materials carried, such as oil or nuclear waste. There are four main classes of marine insurance: hull, cargo, freight, and shipowners' liability.

(*a*) *Hull.* This is insurance cover for damage to the ship itself, taken either for a specific voyage or for a period of time.

(*b*) *Cargo.* Cargo policies may provide insurance for an individual shipment, for regular voyages with similar cargoes, or provide continuous cover by a *floating* policy. Ownership of a ship's cargo depends upon the insurance cover, and may be:

(*i*) FOB (free on board), in which the seller gives up title to the goods upon delivery to the ship; or

(*ii*) CIF (cost, insurance, and freight) by which the seller retains ownership until the end of the voyage.

(*c*) *Freight.* Freight insurance is held against the risk that an owner could incur the costs of transport of a commodity and experience difficulties in actually delivering it.

(*d*) *Shipowners' liability.* This is insurance against damage caused by the actions of the crew of a ship, which might involve claims against the owner, for example, the risk of collision with another vessel, or the mishandling of cargo.

The market for insurance

22. Purpose. The market for insurance brings together buyers and sellers, as well as those intermediaries who facilitate the provision of the service. In Britain insurance is mainly to be found in the private sector and there are therefore associations which safeguard the interests of the parties to the insurance contract. In recent years, however, there has been greater government involvement.

23. Buyers of insurance. The customer may be anyone from a single individual insuring a house contents against theft, or a firm insuring its factory against fire, to a local council insuring itself against accidents to children in a park, or a local charitable organization guarding against the possibility of rain on a day's fund-raising event.

24. Sellers of insurance. Insurance companies can be classified as *proprietary companies*, *mutual societies*, or *industrial life offices*. London is the largest insurance market in the world and 75 per cent of British insurance is conducted abroad as Britain is the base for many foreign companies. Lloyd's of London is a world market for international insurance of all kinds (*see* **30**).

(*a*) *Proprietary companies*: usually companies which provide a wide range of insurance services and are registered under the provisions of the Companies Act, 1985, raising their capital from shareholders.

(*b*) *Mutual societies*: mainly found in life assurance, with the society being owned by the policyholders, raising only sufficient income for the running expenses of the organization.

(*c*) *Industrial life offices*: sometimes referred to as home service offices, usually selling insurance by house-to-house collection of premiums by agents.

(*d*) *Lloyd's of London* (*see* **30**).

25. Intermediaries. In addition to buyers and sellers, there are also *intermediaries* who operate in the insurance market.

(*a*) *Brokers.* Insurance companies obtain much of their business from brokers who operate from their own premises and advise clients on the insurance cover best suited to their needs. Brokers receive payment in the form of commission from the insurers when clients take out a policy with them on that advice.

(*b*) *Agents.* Industrial life (or 'home service') companies have always depended upon agents – part-time and full-time – to sell insurance by visiting customers. Bank managers, solicitors, and estate agents are also people in positions in which they can advise clients upon insurance cover, and obtain a commission from insurers for acting on their behalf.

Lloyd's of London

26. The market. Lloyd's share of the world's insurance market confirms its reputation as the leading international market for most forms of insurance other than life insurance. It exists only as a market – a building which provides facilities for the business dealings of its members. The actual business of insurance is conducted by *underwriters* who have been granted membership by satisfying the Corporation of Lloyd's that they are of sound financial means (assets of at least £200,000 have to be shown).

27. Development. The origins of Lloyd's extend back to over 300 years when merchants used to gather in Thomas Lloyd's coffee-house to underwrite one another's business ventures by agreeing to pay a sum of money if financial losses were incurred. A unique feature of membership of Lloyd's is that every member has to accept individual and unlimited liability, so that if losses are made on insurance provided by them, they are liable for the whole amount of their wealth. Nevertheless, becoming a 'name' has obvious attractions and membership has continued to increase – to 33,500 in 1988 – although fewer than 6,000 will be 'working names' employed full-time upon insurance business at Lloyd's. In recent years membership has been extended to companies, women, and foreigners.

28. Syndicates. Underwriters organize themselves into *syndicates* (400 in 1988) within which one member is usually empowered to accept business on behalf of the group. Syndicates usually specialize in one form of insurance.

29. Lloyd's brokers. Underwriters do not deal directly with the public. Clients are represented by approved Lloyd's brokers who obtain quotations from underwriters (as well as from sources outside Lloyd's) and then place business with those offering the best terms.

30. Lloyd's reputation. The name of Lloyd's – a byword in insurance the world over – is based upon a reputation built over centuries for reliability, integrity, and a willingness to undertake new risks. Its range of business is phenomenal – from supertankers and satellites to a singer's voice or an athlete's legs. But in recent years its reputation has suffered a number of setbacks.

(*a*) In 1979 the Sasse syndicate paid out over £20 million on fire damage to property they had insured in New York. Arson was suspected and they challenged Lloyd's right to insist that payment should be made.

(*b*) In 1982 the Howden syndicate was accused of misappropriation of funds and its lead underwriter was suspended.

(*c*) In 1985 the PCW syndicate was found to have diverted funds to private use and one of its members was expelled.

These and other crises obviously endanger Lloyd's reputation and in 1982 the Lloyd's Act was passed. By vesting certain statutory powers in the Council of Lloyd's, the Act provides an overall framework within which a flexible system of self-regulation can continue to operate.

Regulation and control

31. The Association of British Insurers (ABI). The ABI is the central trade association representing the major insurers. It has over 300 member companies.

32. Ombudsman. The Insurance Ombudsman Bureau was established in 1981 to adjudicate on complaints made by the public against insurers. The bureau is supported by most of the major insurance companies, and although it has powers to order an insurer to pay out any amount up to £100,000, both companies and customers have proved willing to accept judgements made.

33. The role of government. The British insurance industry has traditionally existed largely in the private sector, with a minimum of goverment intervention – unlike most European countries in which the industry is closely regulated by the State. This freedom has allowed insurers to undertake new and challenging risks as they appear and to provide business with the service it needs. The difficulties of some insurers in the 1970s, however, meant that self-regulation was no longer adequate and made governmental intervention essential. The Insurance Companies Act, 1974 was an important move towards official supervision of the insurance industry by the government, and introduced the requirement that new insurance companies must have a minimum capital base of at least £121,000.

Procedure

34. Taking out a policy. Insurance cover is in the form of a contract – a legally binding agreement between the insurer (the *first party*) and the client (the *second party*), and may involve a *third party* to whom the client has a duty or responsibility. The contract comes into being in the following way.

(*a*) An ENQUIRY is made to an insurer or via a broker or agent.

(*b*) An application for insurance is provided by a PROPOSAL in which the client provides information upon which the insurer can assess the risk.

(*c*) The insurer makes an offer to provide cover by stating the cost – the *premium*. The client's payment of this brings a legally-binding contract into being.

(*d*) A *Cover note* may be issued as evidence that the insurer has accepted the risk but that full details are incomplete.

(*e*) The agreement between the insurer and insured is then issued in the form of the *policy* which gives full details of the nature of the risk and the conditions.

(*f*) A *renewal notice* is usually sent by the insurer just before the expiry of the period of insurance and gives details of the premium payable for its continuation. '*Days of grace*' may be allowed by the insurer for a time during which cover may continue whilst awaiting payment.

(*g*) If a risk insured against should actually occur then a *claim* has to be made, i.e. the client demands that he or she be indemnified by compensation from the insurer to restore the client to his or her position prior to the mishap.

Case 12 Salvage in space

In 1984, Palapa B – a communications satellite launched for the Indonesian government – developed a fault and ceased to function. The satellite had been insured at Lloyd's and claims were immediately made to the underwriters there who had insured it. At the same time another satellite – Westar 6 – had also ceased to function. Together the failure of the satellites represented a total liability of $180 million to the Lloyd's underwriters who had insured them – the biggest loss ever experienced in space.

The satellites had been mainly insured by two syndicates at Lloyd's. The expected response by Lloyd's to the demand by the Indonesian government to be indemnified for their loss was obviously that payment should be made to compensate them. But Stephen Merrett, the lead underwriter of one of the syndicates involved, proposed instead that an attempt be made to rescue the satellites in space. Discussions with NASA – the USA National Aeronautics and Space Administration who had launched the satellites – and Hughes Aircraft, the company who had built them, established that the satellites could possibly be brought back to earth and repaired at a cost of just over $10 million. Whilst the success of the attempt could not be guaranteed, it did offer the hope that a large saving could be made by repairing the satellites and returning them to the use for which they had been intended. The decision was therefore taken to proceed with the mission. The rescue proved successful, to the satisfaction of all – NASA for their technical expertise in making the rescue, Hughes Aircraft for repair of the satellites, and – most importantly – the Lloyd's underwriters who were able to recoup a considerable amount of money paid in compensation. Lloyd's recognized the achievements of the astronauts by awarding them the Lloyd's Silver Medal – presented by the President of the USA.

Progress test 12

1. Define insurance. (**1**)
2. Distinquish between insurable and non-insurable risks. (**2**)
3. Explain how insurance works. (**3**)
4. What functions does insurance serve in modern business? (**5**)
5. How important is insurance to business? (**6**)
6. Briefly explain the main principles of insurance. (**7-10**)
7. What are the main types of insurance? (**12-21**)
8. Describe who are the (*a*) sellers, and (*b*) buyers of insurance. (**23-24**)
9. Describe the role of intermediaries. (**25**)
10. What is Lloyd's? How is it governed? (**26-30**)
11. Explain the role of underwriters, brokers, and syndicates at Lloyd's. (**27-29**).
12. What is the role of the Insurance Ombudsman? (**32**)
13. Discuss the role of the government in the insurance industry. (**33**)
14. Describe the procedure for taking out an insurance policy. (**34**)
15. What would have been the expected response from Lloyd's to the demand for compensation? (**Case 12**)
16. Explain why the attempt to rescue the satellites was made. (**Case 12**)

Part four

People and business

13

People and employment

Population

1. Introduction. The effective running of business depends to a large extent upon the organization of a country's human resources. Such factors as the size, age, and sex of the population, may have a considerable influence on business which has to adapt to changes as they occur. It must also be remembered that people are consumers and therefore affect business by their exercise of choice in terms of goods and services provided.

2. The British population. The population of the UK is over 56 million, the 15th largest in the world. The country is densely populated, with 230 people per square kilometre. A number of major cities, such as London, Glasgow, and Leeds have large populations, and in some areas, such as Greater London, West Midlands, and Merseyside, heavily-populated conurbations have been formed by the merging of the boundaries of several towns.

3. Factors affecting population.

(*a*) *The birth rate*. The rapid growth of the British population at certain times, as in the post World War II 'bulge,' has been due to a rise in the birth rate. The birth rate is usually expressed as a certain number of births per 1,000 of the population, and in recent years it has declined as more women take jobs and smaller families become the norm.

(*b*) *The death rate.* One of the reasons for the explosion of the British population in the 18th century was a decline in the death rate, as better public health facilities and improvements in diet helped people to live longer lives.

(*c*) *Rate of migration.* Britain, together with many other countries, is affected by the rate of migration, i.e. the number of people entering and leaving the country. Whilst the numbers of people leaving and arriving here are generally reasonably equally balanced, the nature of the population changes as a result of migration trends. Immigrants are usually young people from the old Commonwealth countries, while those who emigrate are often older and well-qualified people joining the so-called *brain -drain*.

4. The working population. The working population of a country consists of those people in employment or who are seeking employment. In the UK, the working population (27 million, i.e. approximately half the total population) is defined as being those people aged between 15 and 65 who pay National Insurance, and also includes such groups as full-time students and members of the armed services.

(*a*) The *activity rate* shows the relationship between the working population and non-working population. It indicates the size of the working population which has to provide the resources to support those people such as children and pensioners, who are not in employment.

(*b*) The *age structure* of the population is important because it affects the relationship between the working population and the non-working population. An ageing population or an increasing number of children of school age, for example, places an increasing burden upon the working population.

(*c*) The *sex distribution* of the population may be another factor which will affect the pattern of production. In Britain, there has, in the past normally been more females than males as men emigrated or were lost in two world wars, and life expectancy for women has generally been longer.

5. Occupational distribution. There has been a considerable change in the range and nature of jobs in recent years. In Britain, the Department of Employment classifies employment in four main divisions: *primary occupations*, such as mining and agriculture, *manufacturing and construction*, *services*, and the *armed forces*. With continuing economic development, the number of people employed in the labour intensive primary industries has declined to a very small proportion of the labour force, while employment in the service sector in jobs such as banking, insurance, and administration continue to increase, as shown in Fig. 13.1 below.

	1974	**1985**
Agriculture	2.8%	2.7%
Industrial production	42.3%	33.6%
Services	54.9%	63.7%

Figure 13.1 *Changing pattern of employment in UK (%)*

As the nature of jobs has changed so too has the occupational mobility of the country. Whereas at one time a person would occupy one job throughout a working life, today many people have three or more complete changes of occupation within their working lives. The main reasons are as follows.

(*a*) The developing importance of service industries as compared to heavy industry. With rising standards of living, more money is being spent upon services such as health care, education, telecommunications, and leisure, resulting in more employment in those expanding industries.

(*b*) Technological change is also having a major effect upon employment. Innovation throughout industry, based upon computerization and robotization, is resulting in rising productivity and thus the need for fewer people in employment.

(*c*) The rising number of women in employment has been another important development in recent years, following legislation to ensure equal pay and opportunity, and also as a result of changing social attitudes. The number of part-time jobs as a mode of employment has increased at the same time, mutually popular with firms and their female employees.

(*d*) The pattern of employment has also undergone geographical change as improved transportation makes it unnecessary for industries to be linked to power sources or raw materials. The present locational trend, therefore, is to the south of the country to more favourable situations close to the markets of the EEC.

6. Unemployment. One of the most worrying features of most advanced economies has been the increase of unemployment during the 1970s, frequently on a long-term basis. The definition of unemployment is not as straightforward as it might at first appear. The International Labour Office defines the unemployed as being those people who, during a specified period of time, were without a job, seeking work, and available for work, and this definition is the basis of unemployment statistics in many industrialized countries, such as the USA. In the UK, however, the number of unemployed is defined as those people who claim unemployment benefit, supplementary benefit, or National Insurance credits. Unlike other countries, therefore, Britain includes within the calculation of the unemployed those people who, because of illness may not be available for work, and a further difference is that it is no longer necessary to register for work to obtain benefits.

People in employment

7. Contract of employment. A contract of employment comes into existence when an offer of employment is received and is accepted. Whilst all the details of the job are part of the contract, the employer is legally responsible for ensuring that an employee receives a written contract no later than 13 weeks after starting work. The Employment Protection (Consolidation) Act, 1978 provides a number of safeguards for employees and requires that the contract includes certain details, for example, pay, hours of work, and pension.

8. Termination of the contract. The contract of employment can be brought to an end by either the employer or employee. The period of notice to be worked is usually contained in the contract or may be assumed from the pay arrangements – weekly paid staff are assumed to be entitled to a week's notice whilst employees paid monthly are entitled to, (or are required to give), one month's notice. The Employment Protection (Consolidation) Act sets out minimum periods of notice which apply to all employees who have completed at least four weeks with an employer.

9. Dismissal. An employer can dismiss an employee subject to giving the minimum period of notice as described above. In some cases, however, such as dishonesty, serious neglect of duties, or absence without good reason, an employee can be dismissed without notice. In such cases the employer has to ensure that he or she has acted fairly, as an employee who feels that he or she has been unfairly dismissed can bring a complaint before an industrial tribunal. If a dismissal is found to be unfair, a tribunal can order reinstatement of the employee to the job, or award compensation.

10. Redundancy. An employee may become redundant when dismissal is a result of a job ceasing to exist, for example, by a firm's loss of business or closure of one of its shops or factories. A redundant worker who has been employed by a company for over two years becomes entitled to redundancy pay, depending upon age and length of service. Redundancy can often be guarded against by careful forecasting of manpower needs, by providing for early retirement, or by a lower level of recruitment. In a situation where redundancies are likely to occur, a company has, by law, to take certain steps, such as consulting with trade unions involved and by seeking all possible means of reducing the number of redundancies.

11. Resignation. A contract of employment can be brought to an end by an employee tendering notice to the employer.

12. Retirement. A working life normally ends in retirement. The normal retirement age for men is 65 and for women 60, and a retirement pension is usually paid.

Conditions of employment

13. Safety. Employers are responsible for ensuring that workers are protected against all reasonable risks. Legislation over a long period of time has made provision for such factors as the handling of dangerous materials, precautions needed for using some machinery, and for ensuring means of evacuating buildings if necessary. The Health and Safety at Work Act, 1974 outlines general principles regarding workers, as well as the general public, and makes provision for detailed regulations to be made within it. The Health and Safety Executive which was established by the Act is responsible for enforcing legislation and for inspecting premises. Legal action can be taken against an employer who fails to make adequate precautions for the safety of staff, and individual employees can also take legal action, for example, for damages if an employer has been guilty of negligence. State benefits for injuries at work are also available.

14. Health. The provision of first-aid and medical services is essential at a place of work and the Health and Safety at Work Act, 1974 details general principles of health and hygiene.

15. Working conditions. Legislation requires that the workplace satisfies a number of conditions such as the provision of adequate heating and lighting. The hours of work of many employees are regulated by law, for example for women and young people in factories, lorry drivers, and miners. Organization of work has changed considerably in recent times as firms have introduced such practices as shift working and flexible working hours which make more productive use of equipment and offer employees the opportunity to organize their own working life. Normally referred to as *flexitime*, there are a number of variations, such as staggered starting and finishing times or varying break periods, and schemes may allow for holidays to be taken when sufficient hours have been worked during a certain period.

16. Welfare. Most firms seek to provide for the well-being of their employees by the provision of various facilities. A large factory may, for example, have a sports and social club, or a large national organization may have its own journal, while informal points of contact between the organization and its staff exist in most firms.

Pay

17. Introduction. The main forms of payments to employees are:

(*a*) wages, or
(*b*) salary.

Wages are usually paid as a certain sum per hour to manual workers, while a *salary* is a fixed annual sum which may be paid monthly to non-manual staff.

18. Calculation of wages

(*a*) The most usual payment is on a *basic time rate*, often agreed by negotiation between trade unions and management. Pay is expressed as an hourly rate.

(*b*) A *flat rate* may be paid, calculated on the basis of a set number of hours to be worked during a week.

(*c*) *Shift pay* may be paid to employees who work shifts at 'unsocial' hours such as night-time.

(*d*) *Piece rates* were once a feature of manufacturing industry whereby earnings were calculated upon the basis of units of work completed. This means of calculation is sometimes used today as a *payments by results bonus*.

In addition, there may be supplements earned, such as overtime payments, danger money or dirty money for work in exceptional circumstances, cost-of-living allowances to employees in high-cost areas such as London, and long-service payments for unbroken employment with one firm.

19. Salary. A salary is usually expressed as a fixed annual sum, and it is not usual for other payments to supplement it, although certain additional benefits may be provided (see 22 below). It is usual for a salary to be calculated on a progressive scale in which annual increments are made.

20. How payments are made. Payments to employees are usually expressed as *gross* pay, i.e. the total amount paid by the firm. The amount received by the employee after various deductions have been made is the *net* pay. The deductions made are *statutory* deductions, and *voluntary* deductions.

(*a*) Statutory deductions are imposed by law and are therefore compulsory:

(*i*) income tax: deducted by the PAYE (pay as you earn) system.

(*ii*) National Insurance, which is the employee's contribution to state welfare, for example, for pensions and health-care.

(*b*) Voluntary contributions, which may be, for example, payments to private medical schemes such as BUPA, union membership fees, or savings schemes.

Payments to employees can be made by cash, cheque, or credit transfer. Payment is always accompanied by the *pay advice*, which details the various payments and charges made. The most important items of information for the employee are the gross pay, the various deductions made, and the net or *take-home* pay. Any additional payments such as overtime are listed, together with items such as the employee's National Insurance number and tax code. Most pay advice forms today are computerized and information is available promptly.

Two tax forms are of importance:

(*a*) P45: when an employee starts a new job, details of the amount of tax paid up to that time are shown;

(*b*) P60: which is an annual statement of tax paid during the year.

21. Pay legislation. Some of the most important items of legislation relating to pay are as follows.

(*a*) The Equal Pay Act, 1970 provides for equal pay to be made to men and women engaged upon similar work in the same employment.

(*b*) The Sex Discrimination Act, 1975 makes discrimination by an employer on the basis of the sex or marital status of the employee illegal.

(*c*) Employees who are laid off from work or have been put on short time if insufficient work is available for them are guaranteed their pay for a certain period by the Employment Protection (Consolidation) Act, 1978. This act also provides for maternity pay to be made to employees and guarantees a subsequent return to the job.

22. Fringe benefits. Many jobs have financial advantages in addition to earnings. Such fringe benefits or *perks* are usually of goods or services such as a company car, membership of a private health scheme, or of a company's own pension fund. In order to attract the right people to a job a firm may offer help with removal expenses or to provide a low-interest mortgage for house purchase, and recently share ownership and profit sharing have become popular in recruiting and keeping staff. Low-priced meals in a firm's canteen is sometimes another advantage, or possibly the provision of luncheon vouchers by smaller firms.

Motivation

23. Introduction. An important aspect of the management of human resources in business is that of ensuring that employees are motivated to perform the work for which they have been employed efficiently. At one time it would have been assumed that satisfactory wages and job security would have been sufficient motivation for workers, but today a number of other factors are recognized.

24. Needs. Everyone has a range of needs and is motivated in various ways to seek satisfaction for those needs. Human needs have been divided into the following classes by A H Maslow, the Amercian psychologist.

(*a*) The basic needs of food, warmth, and shelter.

(*b*) Safety needs, such as protection against harm, or the unexpected, and which would include job security.

(*c*) Social needs, for example, the feeling of belonging to a family or group at work.

(*d*) Esteem needs by which a person seeks recognition for achievement.

(*e*) Fulfilment needs to satisfy one's potential fully.

Maslow suggests that people move from satisfaction of basic needs to more ambitious objectives. Thus, the basic needs for food and shelter may be satisfied by getting a job at a fairly low wage, and interest is then shown in higher needs, such as the motivation of a job with additional benefits such as a company car as evidence of status.

Two opposing views of the behaviour of employees were proposed by Douglas McGregor, the American writer. His *Theory X* was the traditional assumption of the employee's dislike of work and thus the need for control. His *Theory Y* took the opposite view of assuming that workers enjoyed work and would seek fulfilment of social and esteem needs. The acceptance of Theory Y by management obviously requires a completely different approach in which motivation is provided in various ways to encourage workers to undertake responsibilities and satisfy needs.

25. Work and satisfaction. Our understanding of the word *work* is that of an activity directed by others by which we participate in producing goods or services and for which we are paid. Our needs, as defined by Maslow above, can be satisfied to greater or lesser extent by work, from simply securing a basic standard of living to enabling us to achieve complete fulfilment of our potential. Some people may be satisfied with a steady job at a reasonable wage in satisfactory working conditions. Others may value the friendship of colleagues at work, a position in which authority may be exercised, or the opportunity to employ one's creative talents. The changing nature of the working environment is making it more necessary than ever that opportunities are sought wherever possible to ensure job satisfaction.

26. Job evaluation. To ensure that jobs are fairly paid in relation to one another within a firm, the demands and requirements of each job is evaluated. Job evaluation can then provide a basic pattern for jobs within the organization by considering such factors as working conditions, difficulty, and training required. Jobs are then ranked in order of value and may be organized into grades to simplify the pay structure.

27. **Merit rating.** It is important also to have a system of appraisal of workers' performance, so that increases in pay may be awarded, training needs highlighted, or a move to another job indicated. Usually, a system is developed whereby employees are divided into grades based upon merit.

28. **Management by objectives (MBO).** MBO has been developed as a means whereby the ambition of the employee can be integrated with the objectives of the firm. Management and workers agree together upon objectives which can then be reviewed after a period of time.

Case 13 Employment in the hotel and catering industry

The hotel and catering industry offers a wide range of employment. It is a large industry – it is estimated that nearly 2.5 million people are employed, amounting to almost 10 per cent of Britain's total workforce. Employment is growing at about two per cent a year, with the increasing popularity of tourism and the growth of the service industries generally. About 120,000 jobs for young people are produced by the industry every year, and nearly a quarter of all jobs are in the London area. As might be expected by the nature of the industry, a large proportion of the jobs are part-time – 62 per cent compared to 38 per cent full-time jobs. It is also an industry which provides wide opportunities for women, who make up 73 per cent of the employees – over a half of the managers, supervisors, and proprietors are women, compared to only 20 per cent in business and industry generally. The other main feature of the industry is the number of people who are self-employed, many as proprietors of small hotels and guest houses.

Employment in the industry is spread over a number of main sectors. About 16 per cent of the industry's workforce are employed in hotels – the sector which is growing most rapidly. The hotels sector includes a variety of types – from a large number of small guest houses to some large groups such as Trust House Forte with its chain of 200 hotels in Britain alone. Restaurants – including the popular fast-food chains, ethnic restaurants (Italian, Greek, and Chinese), 'take-aways', fish-and-chip shops, and snack bars – have about 13 per cent of the industry's employees. Nearly a quarter of the industry's workforce is employed in pubs, clubs, and bars, and a similar number work in the public sector, often in canteens serving the needs of workers in administration, the health service, and education. Employees in the hotel and catering industry are usually classified as being either operational staff or supervisors and managers. Operational staff may be employed over a range of activities – in food preparation, for example, as kitchen assistants, cooks, or chefs; in food and drink service as bar staff or waiting at table; or a variety of other jobs such as chambermaid, receptionist, or porter. With the growth of the industry, promotion prospects to supervisory and management positions have been good in recent years.

A wide range of training opportunities exist in hotel and catering. Entry to the industry can be without any formal qualifications, and training on full-time and part-time courses such as the BTEC National Diploma in Hotel, Catering and Institutional Operations, and City and Guilds courses, are available. The Hotel and Catering Training Board is the industry's training body, and provides information on vocational education and training opportunities.

Progress test 13

1. What factors affect the size of the British population? (2)
2. What is the 'working population'? (4)
3. Explain the changing job structure in Britain. (5)
4. What is a contract of employment? (7)

5. How can it be terminated? (**8**)
6. What is redundancy? (**10**)
7. What conditions of employment do you consider important? (**13-16**)
8. Distinquish between wages and salaries. (**17,18**)
9. In what ways may wages be calculated? (**17**)
10. Explain *gross pay* and *net pay*. (**19**)
11. What are (*a*) statutory deductions, and (*b*) voluntary deductions? (**19**)
12. What are *fringe benefits*? (**21**)
13. What is the importance of recognizing workers' needs? (**22**)
14. Define (*a*) job evaluation, and (*b*) merit rating. (**24,25**)
15. Describe the employment opportunities in hotels and catering. (**Case 13**)
16. What are the main features of employment in the industry? (**Case 13**)

14

Recruitment, selection and training

Recruitment

1. Introduction. People are a vital resource for business, and the function of securing the best employees for an organization and providing for their training needs is essential in ensuring that human resources are used effectively. Personnel management is that aspect of business which is concerned with the role of people within an organization, and it includes the need to forecast and assess changing manpower and skill requirements.

2. Assessing the need. The continuing examination of the manpower requirements of the firm is an important aspect of its overall strategy in terms of its objectives and future development. Consideration has to be made of a variety of factors, such as the availability of certain types of skilled labour and training needs. In order that the organization's needs for labour are matched by a supply of people able to fill the vacancies, a business uses three techniques: *job analysis*, *job description*, and *job specification*.

(*a*) *Job analysis*. A job analysis is a detailed examination of jobs within an organization. It is based upon study of the main characteristics of each job and the requirements of the person who is employed in that job. The investigation has to depend upon a variety of methods such as interviews with staff and comparisons with previous records of performance.

(*b*) *Job description*. From the job analysis, a job description can be developed. This specifies the purpose of the job, the work to be performed, skills needed, and responsibilities.

(*c*) *Job specification*. This is a statement of the requirments of the job, describing the qualifications required of the person needed to fill it. Such details as experience needed, training requirements, and specific skills involved are all important in drawing up a job specification which ensures that the most suitable people can be recruited.

3. Sources of recruitment. Following upon preparation of the details and requirements of a job, the next step is the recruitment of suitable personnel. The process of recruitment involves consideration of a vacant job, the available sources for recruitment, and the means by which applicants can be attracted.

(*a*) *Internal sources*. The first step in filling a vacancy may well be for a firm to look amongst its own employees for a suitable person. Hiring from within an organization is becoming increasingly popular as extensive details are held of employees' qualifications, and as internal promotion also contributes to good morale.

(*b*) *External sources*. Whether a vacancy is a result of the need to replace someone leaving the firm or is to fill an additional position, it is obviously necessary on occasions to recruit people from outside. A variety of sources can be used by the firm.

(*i*) Government agencies. A national network of Job Centres is run by the Training Commission which provide details of vacancies and general information on employment. People who are unemployed can register and look for work at their local Job Centre, which provide firms with a simple and inexpensive means of recruiting labour. More specific needs in terms of professional and technical personnel are met by the TC's Professional and Executive Register, and a resettlement service for disabled people is also provided. Local education authorities provide a career service for young people, while many firms have their own contacts with schools, colleges, and universities.

(*ii*) *Private agencies*. An increasing number of private employment agencies provide a source of labour for firms. The most popular occupations are those catered for by office staff bureaux, especially clerical, typing, and computer staff. Staff recruited, usually on a temporary basis, are paid by the bureau from fees paid to it by the firm. Another important role is fulfilled by those private agencies specializing in engaging senior staff for firms. The agency usually undertakes the whole recruitment process and recommends suitable candidates to the firm. This form of *head-hunting* is inevitably expensive.

(*iii*) *Trade unions*. For some jobs, especially in skilled trades, registers of members kept by trade unions can be a useful source of labour for a firm.

(*iv*) *Professional bodies*. Appointments to professional positions are often made as result of reference made by a firm to a register of members kept by a professional association or by advertisements in an association's journal.

(*v*) *Advertising*. An advertisement placed in a newspaper, magazine, or trade journal is a firm's most usual way of notifying possible recruits of vacancies in its labour force. The advertising columns of many papers and periodicals are dominated by the *situations vacant* section, ranging from large block advertisements for senior personnel to a range of tightly-worded *small-ads* for part-time staff. The high cost of advertising makes it imperative that a firm is able to attract suitable applicants for its vacancies, and advertisements frequently carry references which enable them to test the effectiveness of the form of advertising it uses. An advertisement has to be clearly expressed in order to provide the firm with a suitable list of applicants with which it can begin its selection procedure. Too many would involve time-wasting scrutiny and rejection of unsuitable applicants, while too few might not provide sufficient choice from which to select. An ideal advertisment for a job vacancy outlines the job specification, and includes the job title, nature of the duties and conditions of employment (for example, wages or salary), experience needed, and training provided, as well as the procedure which should be followed by applicants.

Selection

4. Definition. The next stage in filling a vacancy is that of selection, whereby the firm takes its assessment of the applicants and makes its choice and offer of employment.

5. Application. All candidates are normally expected to either write a letter of application or, more usually, to complete an application form drawn up by the firm. If the application is in the form of a letter, it is usually accompanied by a curriculum vitae (CV) providing information such as age, education, qualifications, and experience. This information, together with recommendations from people who are able to support the application in the form of *testimonials* (written declaration of the candidate's suitability) or as *references* obtained directly by the firm, then becomes the basis upon which the selection process rests.

6. The shortlist. The firm then starts the *screening process* by which candidates' qualifications and suitability are evaluated. Information provided by the application form and references are looked at to determine whether each applicant meets the requirments of the post, and a shortlist of candidates to be interviewed is drawn up. It is at this stage that candidates who it is felt do not satisfy the requirements of the vacancy are notified in writing by the firm.

7. The interview. The first formal contact between the applicant and the firm will normally be at the interview. The purpose of an interview is primarily for the firm to make an assessment of the prospective employee's personality and fitness for the post, but it is also a valuable point at which the candidate can obtain fuller details of the job. Interviews vary in type and may be with a few senior people or with a large panel of people. They may range in nature from a routine questioning of details in the application form, to a *stress* interview, intended to determine the candidate's reaction to a more challenging interrogation.

It is important that thorough preparation is made by both the applicant and the firm. For the candidate, it will be vital that factual questions can be answered with authority and that any queries regarding the nature of the post can be put clearly. Interviewers will need to ensure that any details necessary for them to arrive at the selection of the right candidate for the job have been resolved and that they in turn have been able to provide each candidate with full details of the post.

8. Assessment. After the interview, a systematic appraisal of the qualities and suitability of each candidate is made, and an objective decision sought regarding the best choice for the vacancy. Decisions are sometimes made and candidates notified immediately, or a short period of time may be allowed for further deliberation.

Legislation has been passed in recent years to promote equality of opportunity and to avoid discrimination in employment. The Equal Pay Act, 1970 provided for equal pay and conditions for men and women for work which is broadly similar, while the Race Relations Act, 1976 makes it unlawful to discriminate on the grounds of colour, race, nationality, ethnic or national origins. By the Sex Discrimination Act, 1975, and later by the Sex Discrimination Act, 1986, all discrimination between men and women in terms of hours of work has been removed (with the exception only of nightwork). The Equal Opportunities Commission and Commission for Racial Equality have powers to investigate discrimination.

9. Decision. When the final choice has been made the successful candidate receives an offer of the job. When the decision is made immediately following an interview the offer may be verbal, which, if it is accepted, is then followed by a formal written offer. The written offer will normally be a formal statement of the conditions of employment, which have to be accurately stated as they form the basis of the contract of employment. A medical examination may be included as part of the selection process.

10. Taking up employment. By the Employment Protection (Consolidation) Act, 1978, all employees must receive a statement of their conditions of service within thirteen weeks of starting in a job. Many other details and aspects of the job, such as pension rights, might be brought to the attention of the new recruit at this time.

Most firms now set aside a short period of time at the start of a new employee's service as an *induction period*. This may vary from a very brief introduction to the people and running of an organization to the more sophisticated courses of larger firms which are the start of the employee's training in a new job.

Training

11. Purpose and importance. People are the most important resource of the business, and therefore it is important that employment in the organization should be followed by consideration of the training needs. By a systematic consideration of training needs, it is hoped that there will be a number of benefits for both the organization and the employee:

(*a*) increased output and quality of work;
(*b*) job satisfaction, less absenteeism, and lower turnover rate;
(*c*) wider range of skills and easier adjustment to change;
(*d*) a safer working environment;
(*e*) better promotion prospects.

The current working environment is experiencing rapid change in methods and equipment, and so training has become a vital factor in ensuring that the labour force has the skills and abilities to utilize new developments. In Britain, new developments in training in recent years are seeking to create a more flexible labour market as part of a long-term strategy to reduce unemployment and promote economic growth.

12. Types of training. A number of forms of training are now in existence, including school and college based schemes and training within industry. The National Council for Vocational Qualifications (NCVQ) has been established to develop a framework for the system of vocational courses and to accredit the qualifications of bodies offering awards.

13. At school. Full-time education provides a wide general education which should enable people to develop interests and abilities in certain fields. Hopefully, this will result in the school-leaver finding the sort of employment in which those abilities will be cultivated and ensure that a successful career results. A greater awareness of the school's responsibilities in preparing children for working life has resulted in the introduction of new schemes into the school curriculum.

In 1983 the Technical and Vocational Education Initiative

(TVEI) was established in which a modular course of study would aim to equip pupils with the skills needed by business and industry. Funded and administered by the Training Commission in co-operation with the education service, it became a national scheme in 1987, available in secondary schools in Britain to pupils between the ages of 14 and 18.

In 1986 the Certificate of Pre-vocational Education (CPVE) was introduced to schools and colleges for those pupils intending to stay on in school or college after the age of 16 to prepare for work or for vocational training.

14. At college. Further education offers a wide range of courses for students, both part-time or full-time, mostly of a vocational nature. Students are often supported by their employers who may pay fees or allow time off work. Many students follow courses leading to the award of qualifications by professional bodies, for example, in law and banking, but most courses are now part of a unified national system administered by the Business and Technician Education Council (BTEC). Other courses of a vocational nature are organized by the City and Guilds of London Institute and by the Royal Society of Arts.

Higher education also provides an increasing number of courses of a vocational nature, in addition to traditional degree studies in the main disciplines. Many universities and colleges have developed links with business and industry in recent years and polytechnics were established to foster and develop these links. The Open University (OU) and Open College (OC) were founded in order to make further and higher education available to students on a part-time basis. The Open College enables people to train in a variety of skills using media and local centres. No qualifications are available but the intention is to prepare people for work and provide a means of learning and updating skills.

15. Preparation for work. Many pupils now leave school at 16 to take a place on a Government sponsored *Youth Training Scheme* (YTS). A two year course is provided for people aged 16, and a one year course for those of 17, both schemes combining planned work experience with a period of time spent away from the job at a college. The scheme is employer-based, and caters for those in employment and unemployed.

16. At work. Two main forms of training can be undertaken whilst in employment: *on-the-job* training at the place of work or *off-the-job* training at a specialist centre or local college. In addition to training in specific skills, firms in the service sector have an interest in ensuring their employees attend courses in social skills such as communications, while most firms now also accept the importance of management skills for employees who are employed in a supervisory capacity.

(*a*) *On-the-job training*. For this form of training, the employee remains in his or her normal work situation, and may be simply *learning-by-doing* under the direction of an experienced worker. It is a well-established pattern of training, used, for example. as the basis for apprenticeships to many skilled trades. It allows the employer to retain the services of the trainee during the period of training but can sometimes result in poor methods and practices being passed on.

(*b*) *Off-the-job training*. Some form of off-the-job training is usually essential for more advanced jobs or for theoretical aspects of skills. A period of time therefore has to be spent, possibly at a further education college, specialist training centre, or the firms's own training school. Off-the-job training has the advantage of allowing the trainee the benefit of specialist training under suitable conditions, but may be costly and entails removal from the workforce for a time.

(*c*) *Government involvement*. Industrial training boards, statutory bodies which are government-funded through the TC, operate in seven industries. They were established to provide better arrangements for training in those industries by raising a levy from firms and by giving grants to organizations undertaking training programmes.

The Job Training Scheme provides an opportunity – mainly for young people below the age of 25 – to acquire and develop new skills at skillcentres run by the TC's Skills Training Agency and at colleges. Other training opportunities such as the Training for Enterprise Scheme for business management are provided by the

TC as short, practical courses in basic management skills to encourage participants to set themselves up in business.

Case 14 How NatWest recruits and trains its staff

The National Westminster Bank is one of the 'Big Four' banks, and several thousand new recruits are employed every year. It is an equal opportunities employer, making no distinction between applicants on the basis of sex, race, marital status, or religion. Staff may be appointed to positions at several levels, but most of the bank's needs are met by the recruitment of 16 year-old school leavers, for whom there is no minimum qualification. Academic achievement is obviously an advantage, but the main qualities looked for in a candidate are personality, common sense, and general suitability for working with others in an office environment.

School leavers are employed directly at branches of the bank, usually at clerical grade 1, and may remain at the branch while moving upwards to clerical grade 4. Applicants with 'A' levels or equivalent qualifications such as BTEC are usually appointed to higher clerical grades (possibly grade 3), and are expected to undertake more responsible tasks. Graduates may be recruited to the graduate training scheme, and are expected to earn accelerated promotion into management positions. Graduates with degrees in such subjects as finance or accounting may be appointed directly to higher positions with the expectation that they may become the top managers of the the future.

Basic training is provided for all new recruits by experienced staff at the branch to which they are appointed. Employees can be introduced to most aspects of the work of the bank within the branch, such as dealing with customers, keeping accounts, and procedures for making payments and loans. Training in other aspects of the work of the bank may be organized at divisional level. For example, NatWest has a number of Business Centres at which employees moving to higher grades can gain experience in company finance or in a wide range of other activities such as business development, advertising, or foreign exchange. In addition, there are a number of regional training centres throughout the country at which short training courses and seminars may take place, while courses and conferences for senior staff can be catered for at the bank's own Staff College in Oxfordshire.

Progress test 14

1. How is an organization's staffing needs assessed? (**2**)
2. What are (*a*) internal, and (*b*) external sources of recruitment? (**3**)
3. What are the requirements of a good advertisement for staff? (**3**)
4. What are the main stages of selection? (**5-10**)
5. What is a CV? (5)
6. Explain the procedure for taking up employment. (**10**)
7. What are the benefits of training? (**11**)
8. What are the main types of training? (**12-15**)
9. Distinquish between *on-the-job* and *off-the-job* training. (**14**)
10. Describe the role of the government in training. (**14**)
11. What is an equal opportunities employer? (**Case 14**)
12. What provision does NatWest make for on-the-job and off-the-job training? (**Case 14**)

15

Industrial relations

Introduction

1. Definition. *Industrial relations* can be defined as the relationship which exists between employees and employers. Traditionally the attitude of workers has been to secure and maintain a reasonable rate of pay for their labour – the 'rate for the job'. Management, on the other hand, seeks to minimize wage costs and ensure the maximum effectiveness of human resources within an operation. Industrial relations thus provides the structure, procedures, and institutions which have been developed to determine such issues as rates of pay, conditions of service, and the settlement of disputes which may arise.

The existence of an effective system of industrial relations is an essential feature of industrial societies. It is accepted that a workforce which is contented with its conditions of work will contribute to the efficiency of an enterprise, whilst discontent often results in stoppages which have a high cost to the economy and deters future investment.

2. Industrial Relations in Britain. This depends largely upon a voluntary system of *collective bargaining* whereby employees and employers are organized in trade unions and employers' associations, and negotiations are conducted freely between them. If disagreements between them occur, the services of ACAS, the independent but government-funded Advisory, Conciliation, and Arbitration Service, may be sought.

Trade Unions

3. Definition. Britain has a working population of 27 million, of which 25 million are employees. Employees' interests are represented by trade unions and professional associations, which are formed, financed, and run by their members. Trade unions have been defined as 'any combination of employees, the principal activity of which is the regulation of relations between employees and employers'. Within this broad definition unions play a vital role in influencing working conditions, wages, pensions, hours of work, facilities, production methods, and job specifications – usually by negotiation with management but occasionally through industrial action such as strikes, sit-ins, or by working to rule.

4. Development. Although the association of people engaged in the same kind of work has existed in the past – the medieval craft guilds of weavers, bakers, and masons – trade unions have their roots in the factory system of the 19th century. Skilled craftsmen formed *trade clubs* to secure better wages and conditions but the governing classes were worried at the prospect of powers acquired by them. The Combination Acts of 1799 and 1800 made workers' associations illegal and the transportation of the six farm labourers of Tolpuddle in 1834 shows the dangers faced by early unions. After early initiatives had been taken by skilled workers, the late 19th century saw the development of *new unionism* – unskilled workers combining together to prove that 'unity is strength'. The Trade Union Act, 1871 provided a sound basis for further union development and the period to 1971 has been called the 'century of privilege' when trade unions can be said to have established themselves.

During the 1970s increased union militancy led to calls for tighter legislative controls and the Employment Acts of 1980 and 1982 were passed. Secondary picketing was limited and greater protection provided for the individual in relation to closed shops. The Trade Union Act, 1984 was an attempt to increase democracy in trade unions by encouraging secret ballots, and immunity from legal action would no longer be granted for strikes if a ballot had not been held.

5. Role of unions. The Industrial Revolution brought with it the advantages of specialization and division of labour, but it also meant that workers were dependent upon the factory for their livelihood. Unions therefore developed the vital role of ensuring their members' interests in a variety of ways. Their main aims can be said to be:

(*a*) improved conditions of employment – better wages, shorter hours, and longer holidays;
(*b*) suitable working conditions – adequate heating, lighting, ventilation, health and safety;
(*c*) full employment and national prosperity;
(*d*) job security;
(*e*) benefits for members in case of of sickness, old age, and loss of employment;
(*f*) industrial democracy – participation in the operation of the organization;
(*g*) equal opportunities.

6. Membership. Approximately half of all employees in Britain belong to trade unions. This is a much higher proportion than in other countries such as France (25 per cent), the USA (22 per cent), and the Federal Republic of Germany (38 per cent). There are more than 450 unions in Britain, although the nine largest have 50 per cent of the total union membership in the country. There is a wide range of size, from the largest, (the Transport and General Workers' Union with 1.5 million members) – to the smallest, (the Pattern Weavers Society with only 60 members). Many smaller unions have been swallowed up in recent years in mergers with larger unions. Union membership grew steadily from the 1930s until the 1970s but since then the number of trade unionists has fallen as employment in traditional industries, with well-established unions, declined.

In general, about three-quarters of all unionists have been men but as women have been employed in increasing numbers, the number of women trade unionists is gradually rising.

7. Types. There are four main types of union: craft, general, industrial, and white-collar.

(*a*) *Craft unions* are the oldest type of union with members belonging to skilled trades covering many industries. Members of unions such as the Amalgamated Union of Engineering Workers (AUEW) and National Graphical Association (NGA) usually enter their trades by serving apprenticeships.

(*b*) *General unions* developed out of the *new unionism* of the late 18th century and represent unskilled and semi-skilled workers. Membership extends across industries, for example, workers belonging to the Transport and General Workers Union (TGWU) are employed throughout industry.

(*c*) *Industrial unions* were formed to represent all workers in one particular industry. The National Union of Mineworkers (NUM), for example, includes all types of coal-mining occupation.

(*d*) *White-collar unions* represent workers in non-manual occupations, for example, the National and Local Government Officers' Association (NALGO). Membership of non-manual unions has grown rapidly in recent years and now more than one-third of trade unionists are in this category.

8. Organization. Trade unions are organized at various levels.

(*a*) *Workplace.* Union members within a workplace elect a *shop steward* to act on their behalf as their spokesman in representing their interests to the employer. Although unpaid, the position is traditionally an important one, and many 'unofficial' strikes called by shop stewards caused severe disruption to industry in the 1960s. The importance of the office derives from the volume and range of agreements that can be negotiated with an employer, as the shop steward is the union representative who is immediately available and who is most aware of the operation of the company.

(*b*) *Branch.* The branch is the most important unit of the union in many ways, such as in the organizing of collection of subscriptions and payment of benefits, and in electing delegates to the annual conference. The Branch Secretary is usually a full-time official of the union.

(*c*) *National.* The union's *annual conference*, to which delegates are elected by their branches, has the ultimate power to determine policy. Day-to-day decisions are, however, made by its *national executive council* which provides the main focus of leadership for the union's members.

Unions usually have full-time paid officials, who may be elected by members or appointed by the union. The position of General Secretary is one of considerable importance as a national spokesman for members.

9. The Trades Union Congress (TUC). The TUC is the central body of the trade union movement. It is a voluntary association of over 100 unions, representing 90 per cent of all unionists in Britain. It was founded in 1868 to provide trade unions with political representation and a more unified approach, expressing the collective view of the trade union movement on a range of issues. It has few formal powers over the unions affiliated to it, apart from expulsion, but it exercises considerable influence in trade union matters generally. Its chief functions are:

(*a*) to express the collective view of the trade union movement;
(*b*) to consult with government;
(*c*) to promote the interests of its members;
(*d*) to conciliate in disputes between member unions.

The executive of the TUC is its General Council, elected at the TUC Annual Conference by delegates from the unions affiliated to it.

Employers' organizations

10. Purpose. Many employers join together in employers' associations, usually on an industry basis, for example, the Engineering Employers' Federation. Associations are usually concerned with general trade and information matters relating to the industry, but the main function is that of helping to establish suitable terms and conditions of employment and maintaining good relations with employees.

11. The Confederation of British Industry (CBI). This is the largest employers' organization in Britain, representing 300,000 companies and half the working population. Its role is the promotion of the views of business to the government and to the public at large. It was founded in 1965 as the result of the amalgamation of a number of employers' associations. The CBI fulfils a similar function for its member associations, as does the TUC for its unions, and the two organizations frequently co-operate on industrial matters.

Industrial relations

12. Collective bargaining. The conditions upon which people are employed is largely determined by agreement between trade unions and employers' associations. In Britain this is traditionally based upon an informal and voluntary system whereby employers and unions seek mutually acceptable wages and working conditions. Agreements may be either national or local.

(*a*) *National.* Agreements at a national level are frequently resolved on an industry-wide basis by a permanent body representing unions and employers as a joint negotiating council. The intention of national agreements is to establish basic levels of pay and conditions of employment, as well as to discuss wider issues such as training, safety, and welfare, and these are then supplemented by locally-agreed settlements. Because of the number of workers involved in national agreements, the government may intervene by imposing restrictions on the amount of a pay increase which may be negotiated.

(*b*) *Local.* Collective bargaining also takes place at the workplace, and often considerably modifies nationally negotiated agreements. Local conditions such as a shortage of labour may result in workers being paid a higher wage in that area, and this tendency to wages rising above nationally-agreed levels has been called *wage drift*.

Role of government

13. Responsibilities. It is the responsibility of government to provide the legislative framework for industrial relations, and to ensure that necessary changes are made. In most countries, unions are involved to some extent in the policy-making process. Within the mainly voluntary system of industrial relations in Britain, however, the role of the state is to ensure the conditions by which trade unions and employers' associations can reach agreement.

Breakdowns in communication and procedure do occur, however, and to provide for these eventualities provision has been introduced for:

(*a*) conciliation (a third party seeking to bring both sides together): and

(*b*) arbitration (both sides agree to accept the verdict of a third party).

14. ACAS. The Advisory, Conciliation, and Arbitration Service is an independent, government-funded body to which both the TUC and CBI nominate members. Its function is to encourage collective bargaining and promote reform and improvement where necessary. It can inquire into any industrial relations matter on its own initiative, and its assistance may be sought by management or employees. In addition to the industrial disputes in which it conciliates, it receives requests to provide arbitration by the appointment of either a single arbitrator or board of arbitration.

15. Industrial tribunals. These were established to allow employees to pursue a complaint, such as unfair dismissal or a dispute over redundancy. A tribunal can offer a range of settlements, including the payment of compensation or reinstatement of an employee.

Industrial action

16. Introduction. Disputes and disagreements betweeen employees and their employers are sometimes inevitable, and are usually dealt with within agreed procedures and by collective bargaining. When, however, negotiations between the two sides fail, an industrial dispute may occur. The right to withhold labour is an essential freedom in a democracy and can be used in various ways to bring pressure to bear upon employers.

17. Strike. A complete withdrawal of labour is one of the obvious and well-reported ways of putting pressure upon management.

Action might be a *token strike* for possibly a day in order to indicate the consequences of a longer period of withdrawal. A strike is official if it has the backing of the union concerned, which will probably make strike pay available from its funds to members on strike. A strike may, however, be unofficial (or *wildcat*) if it is called by a shop steward without union backing.

18. Overtime ban. A refusal by workers to undertake additional hours of work can be another important weapon in putting pressure on management. This form of action is particularly effective in industries which depend upon overtime because of irregular hours or shortage of staff.

19. Work-to-rule. Workers decide to apply the rules and regulations of their employment rigidly, thus slowing down work by refusing to use normally accepted short-cuts and working practices. This can be very disruptive in industries where extensive regulations are normally short-circuited in order to ensure smooth operation of the enterprise.

20. Go-slow. Employees perform their tasks at a slower pace than usual and possibly resort to time-wasting methods, but do not break the terms of their contract of employment.

21. Demarcation dispute. Industrial action may result from disagreement between groups of workers or unions about the extent of their responsibilities. In recent years differences between the nature of many jobs have become blurred with technological development, and greater concern has been shown for different levels of pay between jobs.

22. Closed shop. A dispute may arise from the fact that all workers in a firm are members of a single union who refuse to work with non-members.

23. Picketing. Workers in dispute with their firm may stand outside its premises to attempt to deter other workers from continuing at work. This form of action has proved highly effective in disrupting output and recent government legislation (*see* **4** above) has made *secondary picketing* – i.e. workers picketing premises other than their own place of work – illegal.

24. Sit-in. This is sometimes also referred to as a Work-in, when workers refuse to leave their place of work or to allow receipt or dispatch of goods or materials. Workers frequently resort to a sit-in when a decision has been reached to close a plant.

25. Blacking. This is an action which arises from a union's decision not to work in conjunction with other firms or groups of workers.

26. Action by employers. Industrial action may also be taken by employers, the most typical forms being:

(*a*) the *lock-out* where employees are refused access to their work: or

(*b*) the taking out of an *injunction*, for example, to prevent employees continuing an illegal practice.

Case 15 The Wapping dispute

Although Fleet Street has always been the traditional home of the newspaper industry in Britain, it had become hopelessly outdated by the 1980s as other countries introduced computerization in place of the old 'hot metal' form of printing. Many disruptions took place in the industry as print unions fought with management over the introduction of new technology and the number of jobs which might be lost as a result.

In January, 1986, talks which had been going on for some time between News International (which produced papers such as *The Times* and *The Sun*) and print unions broke down. Rupert Murdoch, Chairman of News International, immediately sacked 5,500 print workers and moved the operation to a new plant in Wapping, in London's Docklands, manned by members of EETPU (Electrical, Electronic, Telecommunications and Plumbing Union). The dismissed workers – mainly members of SOGAT 82 (Society of Allied and Graphical Trades) and NGA (National Graphical Association) took strike action (following a ballot of their members), supported initially by the NUJ (National Union of Journalists).

SOGAT and NGA began picketing the Wapping plant, but production continued there and a new system of distribution of papers was introduced. Talks with ACAS failed. News International issued a writ against SOGAT for unlawful picketing, and the union was fined and its assets sequestrated (taken over) by the High Court. The anniversary of the start of the strike in January, 1987 saw violent scenes between police and pickets, but in February the unions advised its members to accept improved offers of compensation from News International. Industrial action which had lasted over a year was finally over.

Progress test 15

1. Define the term *industrial relations*. (**1**)
2. Why is it important for business? (**1**)
3. What is a trade union? (**3**)
4. Describe how unions developed in Britain. (**4**)
5. What are the main aims of trade unions? (**5**)
6. Compare union membership in Britain to that in other countries. (**6**)
7. What are the main types of union? (**7**)
8. At what levels are unions organized? (**8**)
9. What is the TUC? What does it do? (**9**)
10. What is the role of employers' associations? (**10**)
11. Describe the work of the CBI. (**11**)
12. Describe the British system of *collective bargaining*. (**12**)
13. What is the role of the British government in industrial relations? (**13**)
14. Describe the types of industrial dispute which may occur. (**16-26**)
15. Who were the parties involved in the Wapping dispute? (**Case 15**)
16. What action was taken by (a) management, and (b) employees? (**Case 15**)

Part five

Aid and control

16

Aid for business

Introduction

1. Aid for business. The environment in which business operates in the western world is, to a large extent created and regulated by government. Democratically elected governments are responsible for maintaining the legal framework within which individuals, groups, and business enterprises can exist and work together effectively. In most countries the level of intervention in the business life of the country has increased, and today the provision of aid in various forms is an accepted responsibility of government.

In Britain, central government is an important provider of many forms of aid to industry and business, and local government also makes contributions in various ways. In addition, there are a number of private sources of aid.

Central government

2. Introduction. Government involvement in business is inevitable in modern times because of the large scale use of resources and the high proportion of national expenditure made by the public sector.

Support for business may take a variety of forms. The responsibility for ensuring an *infrastructure* which serves the needs of business is accepted by the governments of most advanced economies. An effective system of transport and communications, for example, is essential, and in Britain the provision is largely made by central government who are responsible, (either directly or by nationalized corporations), for roads, the rail network, and the postal system. The advantages to business and industry of a highly-skilled work-force are becoming increasingly important, and depend upon central government expenditure, upon training by the Training Commission, and upon educational developments in the nation's schools and colleges. The maintenance of the infrastructure has become one of the most significant ways in which central government can ensure the existence of a framework within which business can be supported.

3. Organization. In Britain, a number of government departments have responsibilities which involve support of business in various ways, while a number are major consumers of services, such as health and education. The main departments with business responsibilities are:

(*a*) The *Treasury*, which holds the responsibility for overall economic policy. This involves consideration of the need to encourage business, in such ways as changes in taxation or by varying the amount or type of public spending.

(*b*) The *Department of Employment*, which is responsible for employment in general, for example, by ensuring adequate levels of trained labour and maintaining an effective system of industrial relations. Many of these functions are administered by agencies such as the Training Commission (TC) and the Advisory, Conciliation, and Arbitration Service (ACAS).

(*c*) The *Department of Transport*, which oversees the provision of transport facilities such as roads, the railway system, ports, and airports. Agencies such as the Civil Aviation Authority and British Ports Authority are responsible to the Department for individual functions, while the running of some of the services are in the hands of public corporations such as British Rail.

(*d*) The *Department of the Environment*, which oversees planning regulations and requirements in terms of siting and use of business premises.

(*e*) The main department with a specific role in the nation's business life is the Department of Trade and Industry. It has been provided with a new image in 1988 by its title (*DTI — the*

Department for Enterprise) focussing attention upon its responsibility for the encouragement of business activity generally. The implementation of most government policies involving financial support of various types is the function of the DTI and is discussed later (see 5).

4. The nature of central government support. Support for business may take several forms. Financial considerations are, of course, vital and are discussed later, but support may also exist in a more general sense in the form of the provision of information services and by promotional activities:

(*a*) *Information*. Business in the modern world depends heavily upon statistical information. Whilst private sources such as banks and trade associations may provide specific information for businesses, the government is an important source of general statistical and other information affecting business and the economy generally. The Business Statistics Office collects and publishes a comprehensive range of statistics on all aspects of business activity, while the Central Office of Information provides general information on economic and business trends and developments. Her Majesty's Stationery Office (HMSO) publishes a wide range of material at regular intervals, providing economic and business statistics and information, for example, *National Income and Expenditure*. These publications provide up-to-date information on a wide variety of aspects, such as overseas market conditions and currency exchange, and are important indicators of trends in the economy such as the cost of living and retail prices (by the Retail Price Index).

(*b*) *Promotion*. Central government also actively promotes business by the provision of various forms of support services.

(*i*) The *British Overseas Trade Board* (BOTB) co-ordinates government support for exports by offering advice to exporters on foreign markets and opportunities, technical requirements, tariffs, and other aspects of trading with other countries. Assistance for firms wishing to exhibit at overseas trade fairs is available, and liaison with British embassies and representatives overseas ensures British exporters both commercial information and political support.

(*ii*) The *Export Credits Guarantee Department* (ECGD) offers insurance cover to offset financial losses incurred by participating in overseas trade. The insurance cover provided is often not available through normal insurance channels, for example, where losses as a result of political actions such as the imposition of import restrictions may occur.

(*iii*) The promotion of tourism to Britain is the responsibility of the *British Tourist Authority* (BTA), together with the English, Welsh, and Scottish Tourist Boards. As statutory bodies, they administer grants and loans to improve amenities and accommodation.

(*iv*) The promotion of overseas investment in Britain is the role of the *Invest in Britain Bureau*, which provides foreign firms with advice on location. Many USA and Japanese firms have been attracted to Britain in recent years (*see* **Case 16**).

(*v*) A number of *Queen's Awards* are made to recognise and promote business, for example, for achievements in exporting or for technological development.

(*vi*) A greater appreciation of the importance of business to the country is sought by various government initiatives in education. A vocational bias has been introduced into some schemes and pupils are encouraged to obtain work experience in many courses, while an increasing number of teachers undertake periods of secondment in business and industry.

(*c*) Financial support is provided by central government in various ways (*see* below).

Financial support for business

5. Central government. The government supports business directly by various forms of financial assistance to overcome difficulties resulting from technological developments or declining demand, in order to help the economy operate efficiently. Areas suffering from high unemployment, for example, have traditionally received help in the form of financial assistance for firms to encourage their location in those areas, while in recent years the development of the small business sector has also been encouraged by financial help.

6. Regional aid. For a large part of this century, financial help has been given to firms which locate in parts of the country suffering high levels of unemployment. Such areas include the north of England and Wales where old and uneconomic heavy industries like coal, textiles, and steel have declined over the years in the face of foreign competition. Regions in which various forms of financial assistance have been available are designated as *assisted areas* — and further divided into *development areas* and *intermediate areas* depending upon the level of support given.

(*a*) The DTI is the department responsible for administering financial support to the regions, while in Wales and Scotland the Welsh Development Agency (WDA) and Scottish Development Agency (SDA) provide support. The Council for Small Industries in Rural Areas (COSIRA) has the specific task of encouraging economic development in rural parts of the country by providing loans, in addition to advice and various facilities. A similar role is filled in Wales by the Development Board for Rural Wales, and in Scotland by the Highlands and Islands Development Board.

(*b*) The nature of financial assistance has undergone considerable change in recent years. Whereas initially aid was provided in order to help people in those regions by providing work in the industries attracted there,the emphasis in recent years has become the encouragement of self-generating growth in the regions by a more selective use of financial aid.

(*c*) From 1983, regional aid was provided under two main schemes — the *Regional Development Grant* and *Regional Selective Assistance*. Central to policy was that regional policy should 'encourage the development of indigenous potential within the Assisted Areas with the long-term objective of self-generating growth in these areas'. By the White Paper *DTI – the Department for Enterprise* (Cmnd 278) of January, 1988, the Regional Development Grant would be terminated as many of the projects funded by it would have gone ahead without the scheme. Selective assistance has become the main emphasis of government financial help whereby firms have to justify that a project would not proceed without financial assistance from the government. The award of Regional Selective Assistance (typically 10–15 per cent of the total cost) is dependent upon criteria such as the viability of the project, the amount of employment generated, and benefit to the region.

(*d*) New financial measures were introduced in 1988 to encourage small businesses in the assisted areas. Firms employing fewer than 25 employees in development areas can obtain investment grants of up to 15 per cent towards the cost of fixed assets, and innovation grants of 50 per cent for development. Small businesses in the assisted areas can also receive two-thirds of the cost of private sector consultancy.

(*e*) Regional assistance includes help for inner cities by the encouragement of business development, enterprise, and employment. The DTI has the responsibility for co-ordinating the work of the *City Action Teams* and *Inner City Task Forces* in the major cities for the work of urban regeneration (*see* **Case 2**).

(*f*) *Enterprise zones* were introduced in 1980 as locations in which business enterprise would be encouraged by the removal of restrictions and provision of incentives. Twenty-five Enterprise zones were established throughout the UK, and the main incentives offered are:

(*i*) certain tax exemptions, especially from local rates;

(*ii*) 100 per cent tax allowances for new investment in buildings; and

(*iii*) relaxation of many restrictions, for example, planning regulations.

7. Innovation. Innovation is another important aspect of government assistance to business, aimed at encouraging firms to exploit technological opportunities. Selective financial assistance is available for research and development (R & D) leading to the development of new products and processes and is seen as being essential to sustaining a competitive position in world markets. Changes were made in the nature of government support of innovation in 1988 — away from general programmes encouraging use of information technology and towards more specific help, for example, for small firms, and in the assisted areas. Greater emphasis was also made upon long-term research, collaborative programmes between companies, and collaboration with higher education institutions. Future support is also to encourage *technology transfer*.

The *British Technology Group* (BTG) is a statutory body responsible to the DTI for promoting the development of new technology into commercial products. It can fund up to 50 per cent of the cost of introducing new products and processes, and seeks to make a return on its investment by a levy upon sales of the new product or process.

8. Helping small businesses. The usual definition of a small firm is one employing up to 200 workers. Small businesses are becoming a significant sector of the British economy, employing one-third of the work-force and contributing one-fifth of gross domestic product (GDP). Many forms of support for business are now aimed at small firms as they are seen as the main source of new jobs and a new driving force in the economy. Recognition of their growing importance is reflected in such ways as the provision of small factory units and in schemes for innovation and technological development. The main financial forms of help for small firms are:

(*a*) The *Business Expansion Scheme* (BES), introduced in 1983, which offers individuals income tax relief for investment in businesses. The scheme, originally intended to last for four years, was extended indefinitely because of its success in attracting new sources of finance for small companies. It was designed primarily to encourage investment in businesses where there is high risk and potentially high rewards, especially in young and unproven companies. Investment must be new, full-risk, ordinary share capital and must be held for at least five years. Investment has to be either directly in the firm or through a BES approved fund, but the investor owns the shares in both cases.

(*b*) The *Small Firms Loan Guarantee Scheme*, introduced in 1981, provides a government guarantee for 70 per cent of bank loans up to £75,000, repayable over two to seven years. It is another means whereby small firms are able to gain access to funds which otherwise may be difficult to obtain.

(*c*) The *Enterprise Allowance Scheme* provides an allowance of £40 per week for a year to a person previously unemployed who sets up in business and has at least £1,000 to invest.

(*d*) The *Business Improvement Services Scheme* (BIS) is a package of grants from the Economic Community and central government to help small firms in assisted areas. Various forms of financial aid are available.

Local government aid to business

9. Introduction. Local government is playing an increasingly important role in aiding and promoting business. Whilst most of the financial support to regions or to sectors of the economy requiring help have been provided from central government sources, local authorities are acting as catalysts in promoting the various forms of assistance available. Local authorities fulfil an important role in creating an environment favourable to business development in such ways as the provision of education facilities and leisure amenities. Local councils lay great stress upon the quality of life and environmental factors when promoting their localities to business and industry.

The organization and operation of local government has been discussed in Chapter 2.

In addition to local authorities, *local enterprise agencies* (LEAs) — partnerships between local councils and private sector organizations — have developed to provide help for small businesses in such ways as schemes for management training. There are over 300 LEAs, organized under the umbrella of *Business in the Community (BIC)*.

10. Role of the local authority. Local authorities are involved in business and industrial development in three main ways:

(*a*) Local authorities have *statutory* duties, many of which are related to business activities. The application of planning controls and building regulations laid down by Parliament is the responsibility of local councils, and approval has to be granted for planning permission for industrial development or for factory building. Land utilisation for business development is a positive aspect of aid by a local authority, which may be able to offer businessmen fully serviced sites with all essential services such as water and power supply. Other important services provided by local councils are refuse collection and disposal and treatment of sewage, which may include industrial effluent.

Maintenance of roads is also an important local authority responsibility, as good communications are regarded as vital in attracting industry to a locality. Provision of housing by councils is also an attraction to firms moving to a locality and seeking accommodation for its key workers.

(*b*) Local authorities also have an *advisory* function to business, and are able to offer invaluable help in such matters as the availability of loans and grants, local wage rates, and labour relations. Whilst this function may initially be important in attracting firms to a locality, it can continue, and many councils now find that they maintain a constant liaison with firms, especially foreign firms who have become resident.

(*c*) Local authorities are now tending to exercise a more positive development role in such ways as building factories and office accommodation. In many cases, councils have recognised the need to provide employment prospects in new and developing industries by reclaiming and re-developing old heavy industrial sites for use as industrial estates or business parks. One-fifth of all small business units (i.e. less than 5,000 square feet) in Britain have been built by local authorities, and many councils now have development funds — often in conjunction with private firms — to finance this development. This form of provision is becoming increasingly more flexible as councils seek clients for whom they may build purpose-built accommodation, while also being able to erect speculative 'advance' factories in the hope of attracting firms.

Aid for business from the EC

11. The European Community. Set up as the EEC in 1957, the Community now has 12 member nations. Its structure, organisation, and operation has been discussed in Chapter 2.

The EEC was formed in order to create a customs union, within which people, goods, and money could move freely across the borders of the member countries. Expenditure necessary to promote common policies is made from the Community budget into which members pay contributions. Expenditure from the budget is allocated to countries in a variety of ways, especially by the *Common Agricultural Policy* (CAP) by which support prices are paid to the Community's farmers. Expenditure is made from several sources to aid business in the Community, such as the *European Regional Development Fund* (ERDF), the *European Investment Bank* (EIB), the *European Coal and Steel Community*, the *Social Community*, the *Social Fund*, and the *European Agricultural Guidance and Guarantee Fund* (EAGGF).

12. The European Regional Development Fund (ERDF). The ERDF (the main form of aid in the Community for regional development) is intended to correct the most serious regional imbalances in the Community and may be used in addition to national schemes operating within member countries. Finance available from the ERDF is allocated according to a percentage range laid down for each country, and may be used for programmes for improving the infrastructure or for specific programmes such as the promotion of tourism. Grants are paid to the governments of each member country, and may be up to 50 per cent of the cost of investment made.

13. The European Investment Bank (EIB). A self-governing institution, the Bank's capital is subscribed by the member countries of the EC. It is the second largest development bank in the world, and its aim is to stimulate development in less-favoured regions by making loans. Typically, loans are medium or long-term and may be for modernisation of industries or for schemes for developing the infrastructure. Loans may be made direct to borrowers, and are usually less than 50 per cent of the cost of the investment.

14. The European Coal and Steel Community (ECSC). This organization provides financial aid to improve the economic and social conditions of the coal and steel producing areas of the community. Its main aim is to encourage a rational distribution of production and a high level of productivity while at the same time safeguarding employment and avoiding unfair competition. Loans are made at reduced rates and grants awarded, for example, for technical development and redeployment of workers.

15. The Social Fund. Set up by the EC, this was to provide money for retraining redundant workers for new jobs. The finance is in the form of non-repayable grants for various types of training, retraining, resettlement, and job creation schemes. Much of the finance is reserved for schemes within the Assisted Areas, where priority is given to training which guarantees jobs upon completion. Funding is available for public bodies such as government departments, public corporations, and local authorities, as well as for private companies.

16. The European Agricultural Guidance and Guarantee Fund (EAGGF). Aid is paid in the form of non-repayable grants and may be for improvement of the infrastructure of poor farming areas such as uplands, or for schemes for improving the conditions under which agricultural and fish products are processed and marketed.

Private sector aid

17. In addition to the various forms of aid for business available from public sector sources, the private sector also offers financial support:

(*a*) The provision of finance for business by the *banking system* has been discussed in Chapter 5. In recent years banks in Britain have developed schemes for providing loans for business at more attractive rates of interest, e.g. for small business development. Together with this form of financial help, advisory support may also be available. Merchant banks are a traditional source of capital for businesses seeking capital for new business ventures or takeovers, and may continue their involvement with a firm when they have invested in it.

(*b*) *Investors in Industry (3i) plc* is an independent private sector organisation set up to provide financial aid for business. As a private sector group, 3i has to show a profit on investments it makes, and tailors its loans to its individual clients' requirements. It invests widely in businesses of all sizes but its main expertise is in financing small business development.

18. A number of private sector organizations provide other forms of support for business:

(*a*) *Trade associations* representing the firms in a particular industry exist to provide their members with various forms of assistance. In addition to regulating trading practices, they may provide common services and also act as a pressure group in representing members' interests to the government. They are usually involved in negotiating with trade unions in the industry, in matters such as pay settlements and terms and conditions of employment.

(*b*) The *Confederation of British Industry* (CBI) is the central body which represents British business and industry. It acts in an advisory capacity for its members, collating information and statistics on relevant matters, and represents the interests of members to the government. The CBI is represented on such bodies as the *National Economic Development Council* (NEDC), and *Manpower Services Commission* (MSC), and is recognised by the government as an important channel of communication with private sector employers.

(*c*) *Chambers of commerce* exist in most localities, representing firms in a particular area, and providing services such as advice, information, and training courses. Their general aim is the promotion of business and industry at the local level, and the protection of the interests of their members. The central organisation is the *Association of British Chambers of Commerce*, which has international links and is actively involved in seeking removal of barriers to international trade.

Case 16 Why Nissan came to Sunderland

The northeast of England is an area which has been badly hit by the decline of industries such as shipbuilding, mining, and heavy engineering. In addition, the region lost one-third of its manufacturing jobs within only four years in the early 1980s, leaving it an area of high unemploymnent — almost one in five was out of work, many of them young people.

When, therefore, the Japanese car manufacturer, Nissan, announced in 1981 that it was seeking to locate a car plant somewhere in Europe, a number of organizations began making efforts to attract it to the northeast. Nissan was anxious to locate in Europe to avoid import quotas by building cars within the EC's tariff walls. Nissan's requirements were for a fairly large, flat site, with services such as water and energy supplied, with access to the motorway system for ease of comnmunications, and with a seaport nearby for easy transport of materials and finished vehicles. The UK seemed to be favoured by Nissan in its initial search — Britain has a positive attitude to inward investment and the Department of Trade and Industry's Invest in Britain Bureau has been active in promoting Britain as a base for overseas investment.

Within the UK, Nissan looked at over 40 different sites, in most of which government grants would have been available. Eventually, in March 1984, Nissan chose a location on the former Sunderland airport at Washington new town as its site.

There were a number of reasons for the choice of Sunderland. The area met the company's requirements in terms of transport facilities, especially the convenience of port facilities close to European markets, while the region's good record in labour relations played an important part in the decision. The forms of aid provided by various agencies were, however, vital to Nissan's decision. Regional aid from central government in the form of grants was paid — £35 million in selective regional aid, and by 1991 it is expected that the company will have received about £100,000 from the government. Aid from the EC was also available in a variety of forms, such as for product and process development, in addition to the opportunity of obtaining cheap loans from the European Investment Bank and other sources.

Local government also played a significant role in attracting Nissan to Sunderland. Tyne and Wear County Council, Washington Development Corporation, and Sunderland District Council formed a powerful lobby, emphasising the advantages of the area. The North of England Development Council was another public body actively promoting the northeast for industrial development — it has even opened a branch in Tokyo to raise further interest there.

The initial investment made by Nissan was in the form of a pilot plant, employing 500 people — a 'screwdriver' operation mainly assembling the Bluebird model arriving from Japan in kit form.

But by 1991, it is expected that nearly 3,000 people will be employed in building 100,000 cars a year at the plant, over 80 per cent of which will be built from British and European components. In addition to the employment opportunities provided, it is hoped that the Nissan plant will act as a stimulus to other foreign firms to locate in the northeast.

Progress test 16

1. How does central government aid the infrastructure? (**2**)
2. Briefly describe which government departments aid business. (**3**)
3. Explain the nature of central government aid for business. (**4**)
4. Why is financial aid given to some regions? (**6**)
5. Describe the nature of regional aid currently given. (**6**)
6. Explain how the government supports innovation in business. (**7**)
7. Describe government help to small businesses. (**8**)
8. What role does local government play in promoting business? (**10**)
9. Discuss what aid is available from the EC for business. (**11**)
10. What aid is available from private sector sources? (**16**)
11. Why was the northeast of England in need of assistance? (**Case 16**)
12. Describe why Nissan chose to locate in Sunderland. (**Case 16**)

17

Regulation and control of business

How business is regulated

1. Introduction. Whilst all advanced economies have derived considerable benefit from business and industry, most have found it necessary to impose various forms of control upon business in order to ensure that the interests of everyone are served. The early development of business and industry was in general achieved with a minimum of government intervention, but today there is an acceptance that some form of authority is essential in the public interest.

2. Regulation and control of the business sector. There is a legislative framework of laws which have been drafted over the years to ensure certain standards or to make practices illegal. The government will include within its policy various strategies for effecting controls, for example, by the nature of its spending or by the level of taxation. In Britain many trades and sectors of business accept the need for *self-regulation* and impose their own standards upon the services they provide.

3. Legislation. Many aspects of business are regulated by law. Law reflects the beliefs of society, and changes occur to meet the needs of the people and its government. New laws are constantly being made, existing laws modified, while those which no longer serve a purpose are repealed. All law can be said to be business law, as business is subject to the whole body of law in the same manner as any ordinary citizen. However, there are specific aspects of the law which directly affect and regulate business activity.

(*a*) Most business transactions and dealings have their basis in the law of contract. This has been discussed in 3:24.

(*b*) Legislation is responsible for creating an environment within which business can be regulated. Dangerous and unhealthy conditions in early factories and other places of work, for example, were made illegal by a number of acts dealing with Health and Safety. This has been accepted as an area in which legislation will continue to be necessary to ensure that places of work are satisfactory.

It is occasionally necessary to legislate in order to make changes in other aspects of business life as the need arises. For example, the Resale Prices Act, 1964 virtually abolished resale price maintenance (RPM) whereby goods were sold at prices fixed by manufacturers. Similarly, abuses in the description and pricing of products led to the passing of the Trade Descriptions Act, 1968 which made false descriptions of products for sale illegal, especially false price reductions in sales.

(*c*) People who wish to take legal action on a complaint can bring a case to a court of law. If their circumstances are such that costs may deter them, they can apply for legal aid in order to obtain the services of lawyers. Tribunals exist to which people can bring a case, for example, against wrongful dismissal, and generally provide a cheaper and more effective form of justice than the ordinary courts of law.

(*d*) The office of *Ombudsman* (*Parliamentary Commissioner for Administration*) was created in order to provide a means for the individual to complain and obtain redress from the state. The PCA can only investigate complaints referred to him by Members of the House of Commons from members of the public, and complaints have to be about faults in administration carried out by government departments. After investigation of a case, the PCA reports his findings to the Member of Parliament from whom it was received and also makes an annual report to Parliament, but he has no powers to take action. A Local Ombudsman and a Health Service Ombudsman have also been established to investigate complaints about local councils and the National Health Service respectively.

4. Government policy. The policy of the government of the day is an important factor in the regulation of business.

(*a*) One of the government's most important functions is that of deciding upon the level of public expenditure, mainly by the annual Budget. The level of funding is obviously vital for business in the public sector as it will have an effect upon the resources it can buy and the number of people it can employ. Public expenditure also affects business in the private sector, for example, by the level of demand for goods needed by public sector organizations.

(*b*) Another important part of government policy will be the level of taxation by which funds are raised to pay for services provided by the state. Taxation is an important factor in regulating business as the level of corporate taxation, for example, corporation tax, can determine how much of a company's income is available for such needs as re-investment or for raising employees' wages. The level of personal taxation will have a similar effect upon the amount of disposable income consumers are left with, and thus may determine the level of demand for certain products and services.

(*c*) Government policy on the regulation and control of business is usually clearly defined. In the 1960s, for example, the Labour government created a wide system of regulation of business by such means as statutory controls on prices and incomes. Conservative governments of the 1980s have, on the other hand, sought to remove many of the regulations on business. In recent years, a number of moves have been made towards encouraging the *enterprise* culture by *deregulation* of certain aspects of business. The White Paper *Lifting the Burden* (Cmnd 9571) in 1985 proposed the removal of many regulations which had become outdated and unnecessary, and recommended that any new regulations should only be made if absolutely necessary. A further White Paper *Building Business....not Barriers* (Cmnd 9794) in 1986 recommended further deregulation which would allow business to concentrate upon creating jobs and generating wealth. Finally, the White Paper *DTI—The Department for Enterprise* (Cmnd 278) in

1988 had as its theme the development of enterprise, proposing fewer controls in favour of encouragement of open markets and individual enterprise and initiative.

5. The EC. Member countries of the EC are subject to regulations and controls imposed by the community. The nature of EC regulations has been discussed in 3:8, and most aspects of business are subject to regulations drawn up by the Community. The purpose of the formation of the Community was the development of free trade between member nations by the removal of barriers between them, and other restrictions, such as those affecting the free movement of workers between countries, are also gradually being removed. *Consumer protection*, for example, was felt to be a necessary concern, as the creation of such an enormous market from the amalgamation of twelve countries meant that consumers were presented with a greater variety of goods. Community measures have therefore been adopted in order to ensure that adequate standards are maintained and that action can be taken in consumers' interests.

6. Self-regulation. In Britain, many industries and trades have traditionally imposed their own form of self-regulation upon their activities, rather than formal controls imposed by the state. Self-regulation means acceptance of the need for high moral standards of behaviour within a voluntary code of practice. The City of London, for example, has many organizations developed from craft and merchant guilds, such as the Goldsmiths and Vintners, which supervise many aspects of their trades. Many professions also have their own forms of self-regulation, for example, the Law Society and the British Medical Association, which are empowered to maintain disciplinary procedures. Self-regulation has always been a characteristic of industries such as insurance and advertising, with the *trade associations* playing an important role. The *Association of British Insurers* (ABI), and the *Advertising Standards Authority* (ASA) fulfil a supervisory role in their industries, maintaining codes of practice and providing means of redress for clients who complain.

In recent years attempts have been made to strengthen self-regulation in some industries, and one feature has been the establishment of an *Insurance Ombudsman* and a *Banking Ombudsman*. Both these positions have been created by the industries themselves, and paid for by firms within the industries. The function of both offices is to receive complaints from the public and to seek remedies from the firms concerned. They are a means of providing fair and impartial adjudication between banking and insurance firms and their customers. If a customer's complaint is found to be justified then the relevant banking or insurance organization has to accept the decision.

7. The public and pressure groups. Controls over business may also develop as a result of actions by the public, especially as a result of pressure exerted by *pressure groups*. In Britain, participation in the democratic process of government and decision-making is one of the traditional liberties, and many forms of business regulation have been the result of pressure. In some industries, such as agriculture, the regulatory framework may depend to a large extent upon the close liaison maintained between the Ministry of Agriculture, Fisheries, and Food and the National Farmers Union. At certain times, members within an industry may *lobby* the government for the removal of certain restrictions, for example, the campaign by the Open Shop lobby group and the 'Cheerup Sunday' campaign led by consumer pressure groups to press for Sunday opening of shops.

Regulation of finance

8. Introduction. The need for regulating financial institutions and the financial system generally is accepted by most countries. There are a number of reasons for this:

(*a*) The importance of the financial sector to a country's economy.

(*b*) The need to protect investors.

(*c*) The occasional difficulties of a bank or other financial institution.

(*d*) The importance of international co-operation in finance.

(*e*) The importance of competing in international financial markets.

Regulation of the financial sector in Britain is by a mixture of *legislation* and *self-regulation*.

9. **Banking.** Banking is a vitally important service for business, and the government accepts responsibility for its regulation. The Chancellor of the Exchequer makes adjustments to taxation and public expenditure in the annual Budget and at other times when necessary and ensures that the money supply is sufficient for the needs of business. The government's policies are carried out by the Bank of England — the central bank — which has statutory powers to issue directives to the commercial banks. In recent years the powers of the Bank of England have been increased by the Banking Act, 1970 and the Banking Act, 1985, following failures in the banking system.

10. **Building Societies.** Building Societies are offering a broader range of financial services today than in the past, and are at the same time becoming more closely regulated. Initially they were institutions which took in savings from people wishing to purchase houses, and were organized under the jurisdiction of the Registrar of Friendly Societies. As they began to compete with banks, however, the need for closer supervision was felt necessary and resulted in the Building Societies Act, 1986. The Act conferred powers upon societies to develop services and to become public limited companies if they wished. Supervision of the societies is now the responsibility of the *Building Societies Commission*, and in 1987 the societies established a *Building Societies Ombudsman* to investigate complaints by the public.

11. **Insurance.** Various aspects of insurance are regulated by legislation, such as the liability of employers (Employers' Liability Act) and the requirement for motorists to have Road Traffic Act cover. The industry has been traditionally *self-regulated*, but the difficulties experienced by some insurers in the 1970s led to the Insurance Companies Act, 1974. This was an important move towards official supervision of the insurance industry and gave the government powers such as the requirement that new insurance companies must have a minimum capital base of at least £121,000.

The main trade association representing insurers is the *Association of British Insurers* (ABI). The *Insurance Ombudsman Bureau*, supported by most of the major insurance companies, was established in 1981 to adjudicate on complaints made by the public against insurers. The Bureau has powers to order an insurer to pay out any amount up to £100,000, but both insurers and the public have proved willing to accept judgements made.

Self-regulation is still effected at Lloyd's, in the form of statutory powers vested in the Council of Lloyd's. The problems of some Lloyd's members led to the Lloyd's Act, 1982 which provides Lloyd's itself with greater powers to enforce its own rules for financial discipline.

12. Financial services. There have been a number of developments in the regulation and control of the financial services industry in recent years. The main reasons for this have been:

(*a*) The rapid growth of the financial services industry.

(*b*) Concern about scandals such as *insider dealing* by which people have made profits out of shares bought on the basis of confidential information, often affecting mergers and take-over bids.

(*c*) The *de-regulation* of stock markets by the *Big Bang* to encourage competition has inevitably brought in abuses.

The *Financial Services Act, 1986* set up a regulatory framework for a wide range of financial services in order that people making investments—buying shares or life insurance policies, for example—can be protected from fraud. By it, the Department of Trade and Industry has greater powers to investigate and prosecute in cases of insider dealing and other offences. Anyone engaging in investment business has to be authorized to do so, and authorization will usually be on the basis of membership of an organization which is *self-regulating*. For example, the Stock Exchange (now the International Stock Exchange) is the self-regulating organization (SRO) for the securities markets and has powers to remove authorization or to take action against a firm breaking its rules. The *Financial Intermediaries Managers and Brokers Regulatory Organization* (FIMBRA) is the SRO for the life assurance and unit trust businesses. The *Securities and Investment Board* (SIB) has been established as the overseeing organization with the role of setting out rules to protect investors, and is equipped with legal powers.

Consumer protection

13. Development of consumer protection. The acceptance of the need for consumers to be protected from the dangers of buying goods which are below standard in various ways has a long tradition. In the Middle Ages, sellers of shoddy goods were forced to walk through the streets with the goods hung around their necks, and many old acts of parliament contained measures which aimed to safeguard consumers from the sharp practices of merchants and traders.

At one time it was accepted that the rule in transactions was *caveat emptor* — let the buyer beware — and that it was the buyer's responsibility to make sure that the goods bought were satisfactory to his or her needs. Today however, there is a mass of legislation protecting the rights of consumers and a number of organizations to implement them.

(*a*) The accepted foundation of the rights of the consumer in Britain is the *Sale of Goods Act, 1893* (now replaced by the *Sale of Goods Act, 1979*), which provided consumers with the right that goods bought by them should be what they claimed to be and that if they were not then money spent on them had to be refunded. The Sale of Goods Act, 1979 establishes that goods bought from a trader must be of 'merchantable quality'; be as described at the time of purchase (for example, a 'showerproof' coat); and be fit for the purpose sold (for example, a watch must keep time). If goods are found not to satisfy these conditions the responsibility rests upon the seller to refund the price to the purchaser.

(*b*) The *Food and Drugs Act, 1955* established conditions for the preparation and sale of foodstuffs to ensure that quality would be of a reasonable standard. The *Labelling of Food Regulations, 1973* made it compulsory for products to have the exact quantity of ingredients contained listed on them.

(*c*) The *Consumer Protection Act, 1961* established powers for making regulations in terms of the safety of goods, to prevent or reduce the risk of injury or death. Colour codes for domestic wiring and the provision of guards for heating appliances are examples of regulations which have been made under this act.

(*d*) The *Weights and Measures Act, 1963* made it a criminal offence not to mark the quantity on goods such as tea and sugar which are normally sold in pre-packed form. Weights and Measures legislation was consolidated into the Weights and Measures Act, 1985.

(*e*) The *Resale Prices Act, 1964* abolished the system whereby the price of goods was established by suppliers, and made possible greater competition among shops. Goods are now often advertised at manufacturer's recommended price (MRP).

(*f*) The *Trade Descriptions Act, 1968* made it an offence for a trader to make false claims about goods on sale, for example, about the quality or where they were made. The Act also made it an offence to advertise a false reduction in price on goods.

(*g*) The *Prices Act, 1974* laid down requirements for the pricing of products in order to avoid consumers being misled. For products such as meat, unit pricing was introduced in order that the price per pound could be indicated and thus comparisons made.

(*h*) The *Fair Trading Act, 1973* set up the *Office of Fair Trading (OFT)*, headed by the Director General of Fair Trading, to provide a continuous review of consumer affairs.

(*i*) The *Consumer Credit Act, 1974* established regulations for the various forms of consumer transactions such as hire purchase and mortgage. The aim of the Act is *truth in lending* and it requires that the total credit price of a commodity has to be shown, together with the annual percentage rate of interest (APR) payable, so that people are able to compare costs of credit. Businesses involved in providing credit facilities are required by the Act to obtain a licence from the Director General of Fair Trading. The Act became fully operational in 1985 and now provides a comprehensive system of protection for consumers in most credit and hire transactions.

(*j*) The *Consumer Protection Act, 1987* extends protection of the consumer to three important areas:

(*i*) it introduces *strict product liability* so that consumers do not have to prove negligence when making a claim for compensation for injury caused by dangerous or defective goods;

(*ii*) it provides a general safety requirement, making it a criminal offence to sell unsafe goods;

(*iii*) it also makes it a criminal offence to give consumers misleading price indication about products.

14. Consumer organizations. There are a number of organizations which safeguard consumer interests.

(*a*) *Central government* responsibility for consumer protection is mainly the role of the Department of Trade and Industry, but other departments also have responsibilities, for example, laws relating to food and hygiene are administered by the Ministry of Agriculture, Fisheries, and Food.

(*i*) The *Office of Fair Trading* and the position of Director General of Fair Trading were established to co-ordinate much of the work of consumer protection.

(*ii*) The *National Consumer Council*, established in 1975, has the general brief of watching over consumer interests and promoting those interests nationally.

(*iii*) The *British Standards Institution* (BSI) is an independent body which sets national standards of safety, performance, and size for a wide range of products. There are over 7,500 British Standards and the BSI *Kitemark* is accepted by consumers as an indication of quality and reliability.

(*iv*) The *Office of Telecommunications* (OFTEL) is the independent regulatory body for the telecommunications industry, responsible for promoting the interests of consumers and for encouraging competition.

(*b*) *Local government* responsibilities for consumer protection are generally carried out by the Trading Standards, Weights and Measures, or Consumer protection departments of county councils. Trained inspectors ensure that regulations are complied with, advisory services provided for consumers, and prosecutions can be brought.

(*c*) *Public corporations* have consultative committees which were established by statute at the same time as the nationalized industry was set up. Complaints can therefore be made, for example, to the Electricity Consumer Council, or to the Post Office Users' Council.

(*d*) The *private sector* has a number of organizations looking after consumer interests:

(i) The *Consumers' Association* is the largest private consumers' organization in Britain and its magazine *Which?* publishes reports of tests of products carried out by the organization.

(ii) *Citizens' Advice Bureaux* (CAB) can be found in most localities in Britain, and for many people may be the first step in seeking advice or in making a complaint. Problems are often resolved by discussion of complaints with traders, and specialists such as solicitors can be called upon for advice.

(iii) Many *trade associations* have developed facilities for dealing with complaints about firms in their industry. The Association of British Travel Agents (ABTA), for example, maintains a code of practice and has a fund from which customers can be reimbursed if a member firm fails. The Motor Agents' Association (MAA) was set up to deal with complaints against its member firms about car purchase or service, while the National House Building Council (NHBC) provides warranties to buyers of houses built by its members.

Competition

15. The need for regulation. A number of regulations and controls exist to ensure fair competition and the encouragement of enterprise and initiative. As business develops the appearance of certain abuses are inevitable, and legislation has been found necessary in order to remove or curb them.

(*a*) The development of *monopoly* is one area of business which is scrutinized closely as unfair competition may result and consumers may suffer. The Fair Trading Act, 1973 set up the *Monopolies and Mergers Commission* to investigate and report on the development of a monopoly situation or the possibility of a merger. Guidelines have been set down: for example, a monopoly is defined as the supply of at least one-quarter of all the goods supplied in the country by one firm. Mergers can be referred to the Commission if they are likely to result in a monopoly situation and mergers between newspaper proprietors are specifically catered for in this respect.

The *Takeover Panel* (properly known as the City Panel on Takeovers and Mergers) was set up by firms in the City of London to act as a self-regulatory body to protect the interests of shareholders. During periods which have seen a great deal of merger activity between firms, the Panel has sought to ensure that mergers go ahead according to the *Takeover Code* and that shareholders are not disadvantaged.

(*b*) The existence of various *restrictive practices* by which firms seek to gain unfair advantages over competitors by agreements on prices or by protecting markets has also led to regulations and controls. The Restrictive Trade Practices Act, 1976 requires that certain practices have to be registered with the Director General of Fair Trading who can investigate them and, if necessary, take proceedings in connection with them in the Restrictive Practices Court. A number of restrictive practices can be distinguished, such as own-price agreements by which producers circulate details of their pricing policies so that one can avoid undercutting another, or exclusive dealing agreements which prevent entry to the market of new firms. Resale price maintenance, by which manufacturers specify the price their products should be sold to consumers, is one restrictive practice which has been gradually checked by legislation and is now seldom encountered.

(*c*) The White Paper *DTI—the Department for Enterprise* (Cmnd. 278), 1988 emphasises that the government's role is to stimulate competition and that the basis of future legislation would be the prohibition of agreements with anti-competitive effects, with penalties for breach of that prohibition.

Employment

16. The need for regulation. It has been found necessary to regulate certain aspects of employment in order to ensure that discrimination against workers does not occur. Taking up employment involves creating a *contract of employment*, which imposes duties and confers rights on employer and employee. The Employee Protection (Consolidation) Act, 1978 provides a number of safeguards for employees, and requires that the contract includes certain details such as the rate of pay and hours of work. Some aspects of employment have been specifically regulated:

(*a*) Under the Race Relations Act, 1976, it is unlawful to

discriminate on the grounds of colour, race, nationality, ethnic or national origins. The *Commission for Racial Equality* (CRE) was set up by the Act, and has a code of practice for implementing policies to eliminate racial discrimination.

(*b*) *Equal opportunities* in employment has been achieved by several regulatory measures. The Equal Pay Act, 1970 provided for equal pay and conditions for men and women for work which is broadly similar. The Sex Discrimination Act, 1975 made it unlawful to discriminate on the grounds of sex or marital status in employment, training, or related matters, and set up the *Equal Opportunities Commission*. The role of the Commission is to work towards the elimination of discrimination and the promotion of equal opportunity. The Sex Discrimination Act, 1986 removed all discrimination between men and women in terms of hours of work, with the exception only of nightwork.

Advertising

17. The nature of self-regulation. The need for control over advertising in Britain has been largely met by the self-regulation of the industry itself:

(*a*) The *British Code of Advertising Practice* ensures that all advertisements are 'Legal, decent, honest, and truthful'. It has been drawn up by advertisers, advertising agencies, and the media, who have all agreed to follow it. The *British Code of Sales Promotion Practice* is aimed at regulating all forms of promotion, for example, free offers and the distribution of vouchers and samples.

(*b*) The *Advertising Standards Authority* (ASA) is funded by the advertising industry to make sure that advertisements conform to the British Code of Advertising Practice, and examines complaints from the public.

(*c*) The *Independent Broadcasting Authority* (IBA) subjects all advertisements received to its own Code of Advertising Standards and Practice before allowing them to be broadcast by the independent television companies or independent local radio stations. The advertising of certain products, such as cigarettes and spirits, is not allowed, and there are strict rules about advertising aimed at children or the use of celebrities to promote products.

(*d*) *Mail order advertising*, by which consumers are often invited to return an order form, is now regulated by codes of practice set up by the media concerned. The Association of Mail Order Publishers (AMOP), and the Mail Order Traders' Association (MOTA), which represent many firms trading by mail order, provides for advertisements to be checked and for advertisers to guarantee the return of customers' money if they are not satisfied with products when received.

18. The need for legislation. Concern at the influence of advertising has, however, led to legislation in recent years:

(*a*) The Trade Descriptions Act, 1968 made it an offence for a firm to apply a false description to any goods offered for sale.

(*b*) The Prices Act, 1974 established rules regarding the use of such terms as 'Sale Price' and 'Bargain Offer'.

(*c*) Advertising is also subject to EC rules and directives, which are likely to modify the British system of self-regulation.

Case 17 The Office of Fair Trading

The OFT came into being as part of the provisions of the Fair Trading Act, 1973, with the responsibility for maintaining a continuous review of trading practices in order that both consumers and businessmen are protected against unfair practices. The OFT is a government department headed by the Director General of Fair Trading, and responsible to the Department of Trade and Industry.

The OFT works closely with the Trading Standards departments of local councils to safeguard the interests of consumers. A considerable amount of information for consumers is published by the OFT, and changes in the law are proposed to government as necessary. The OFT encourages self-regulation by helping trade organizations to draw up their own codes of practice, such as the *Photocode* produced by photographic trade organizations which defines statements such as 'free film' offers and details of how consumers can make complaints if necessary. The intervention of the Director General of Fair Trading is sometimes necessary in developing situations, such as the increasing popularity of party-plan selling and selling by phone, in order to seek agreement on such matters as what period of time may be allowed for cancellation of orders. In recent years the administration of consumer credit legislation has been an important aspect of the work of the OFT, which is the body responsible for issuing licences to traders who provide credit to customers.

The OFT is also responsible for monitoring developments which may be restrictive, anti-competitive, or against the public interest. If a monopoly situation is thought to have arisen — i.e. that one firm controls a quarter of the total supply of a commodity — then the Director General can refer the issue to the Monopolies and Mergers Commission. Similarly, mergers between companies can also be referred to the Commission by the Secretary of State for Trade and Industry on the advice of the OFT, if a merger is felt to be against the public interest. Anti-competitive practices, which might have the effect of restricting, distorting, or preventing competition, can also be recommended by the Director General for referral to the Monopolies and Mergers Commission. Details of restrictive trade practices, such as agreements between firms to fix prices or limit production, have to be submitted to the OFT, and can be referred to the Restrictive Practices Court where they can be prohibited if found to be against the public interest.

In March, 1988 new legislation to combat restrictive practices was announced in a government Green Paper — much of the existing legislation concerning restrictive practices is over thirty years old. The practice of registering restrictive practices is to disappear, and the OFT will determine whether or not an agreement in fact constitutes a restrictive practice. The scope of restrictive practices is also to be widened to include professional bodies — including lawyers, estate agents, and accountants, for example—who have previously been exempt. In investigating restrictive practices, the OFT will have the power to enter and search premises, and to fine companies guilty of making agreements to prevent competition up to a maximum of ten per cent of their combined total turnovers.

New legislation is expected in 1989 to implement the green paper proposals, and the OFT is to be restructured and its activities more clearly defined to enable it to fulfil its new role.

Progress test 17

1. Describe briefly each of the main ways of regulating business. (2-7)
2. Why is it necessary to regulate the financial sector? (**8**)
3. Describe how (a) banking, (b) insurance, and (c) building societies are regulated. (**9-11**)
4. Describe recent developments in the control of financial services. (**12**)
5. Note the main acts which provide the consumer with protection. (**13**)
6. Which bodies exist for the purpose of consumer protection? (**14**)
7. Explain why it is necessary to regulate competition. (**15**)
8. What recent steps have been taken to regulate competition? (**15**)
9. Describe the main controls upon employment. (**16**)
10. What bodies are responsible for advertising standards? (**17**)
11. What is the Office of Fair Trading? (**Case 17**)
12. Discuss how it protects consumers and business against unfair trading practices. (**Case 17**)

Appendix 1
Examination technique

Revision

1. Introduction. All students have their own methods of revising and you will certainly have yours. It is likely, however, that you will benefit by spending a few minutes reading this short guide to revision.

Your revision should have three main aims:

(*a*) complete understanding of the subject;
(*b*) retention and recall of the subject;
(*c*) the ability to explain and apply the subject.

Understanding is the key to both the learning and use of a subject. Thus it is understanding which is crucial to examination success and your revision should be designed above all to reinforce understanding. No matter how much a subject may interest you when you actually study it, learning it for an examination can at best be tedious and at worst boring. You must try to lessen this effect.

2. Revision programme. Tedium in revision is caused mainly by reading the same original notes over and over again. This is also unproductive. It is far better to adopt a *positive revision* programme, one which uses your time profitably and enables you to teach yourself. Your *Handbook* is the perfect basis for such a programme.

Revision should be done a chapter at a time. Try adopting the following sequence.

(*a*) *Re-read* the chapter thoroughly.

(*b*) *Make revision notes*. These can consist of no more than the headings in the text with a very brief note about important principles. Take each note in turn and try to recall and explain the subject matter. If you can, proceed to the next; if you cannot, look in your Handbook. By doing this, you will revise, test your knowledge and spend your time profitably by concentrating your revision on those aspects of the subject with which you are least familiar. In addition, you will have an excellent last-minute revision aid.

(*c*) Construct a chart for each topic using the headings in your Handbook. Many people respond well to diagrammatic explanations and summaries which provide an extremely quick and efficient means of revision. You need to think how best to construct them and in doing so you teach yourself and better understand the subject.

Two tips: do not try to include too much on each diagram; and do not try to economize on paper. The impact and usefulness of a diagram depends very much on its visual simplicity. The same applies to revision notes.

(*d*) Prepare concise explanations of key principles that you are likely to need so that during the examination you do not have to think about how to explain something which you probably know well but cannot easily put into words there and then.

(*e*) Answer the progress tests again. You should find a significant improvement in the number of questions that you can answer immediately. This exercise will primarily test your ability to recall and explain facts.

(*f*) Plan answers to the specimen examination questions in the Handbook and any others set by the relevant examining body. Planning answers is often a more useful exercise than actually writing the answer out in full. In planning you have in effect answered the question and writing it out is a largely mechanical exercise. If, however, you feel that you need the practice in essay writing, answer some fully.

Read the notes on answering questions (*see* **3** below) before planning any answers.

The examination

3. Examination technique.

(*a*) Read the examination instructions carefully.

(*b*) Read through the questions and provisionally mark which ones to answer. Take care over your choice. An apparently simple question might have a hidden twist – do not get caught out. Similarly, never decide to answer a question which is in two or more parts on the strength of the first part alone. Make sure that you can answer *all* parts.

(*c*) Make sure you have selected the right number of questions – you get no extra marks for answering more!

(*d*) Remember that the first 50 per cent of the marks for any question is the easier to earn. Unless you are working in complete ignorance, you will always earn more marks per minute while answering a new question than while continuing to answer one that is more than half done. So you can earn many more marks by half-completing two answers than by completing either one individually.

(*e*) Concentrate on displaying your knowledge. There is almost always one question that you are not happy about but nevertheless need to attempt. In answer to such a question put down all you *do* know, and then devote the unused time to improving some other answer. Certainly you will not get full marks by doing this, but nor will you if you fill your page with nonsense. By spending the saved time on another answer you will at least be gaining the odd mark or so.

(*f*) Plan all your answers – this is absolutely vital.

(*g*) If time is running out put down your answer in the form of notes, making sure that every part of the question has some answer – no matter how short – that summarizes the key elements. Don't worry about shortage of time: it is more often a sign of knowing too much than too little.

(*h*) Check through your answers. A few minutes doing this can eliminate many minor errors and give a final 'polish' to your answers.

Appendix 2

Basic accounting principles

1. Definition. Accounting can be described as the activities involved in the systematic recording and analysis of the financial affairs of a business. A distinction may be made between Book-keeping, the recording of transactions by the business, and Accounting, which is the analysis and appraisal of the finances of an organization. A further distinction may be made between Financial Accounting, reporting upon financial matters, and Management Accounting, which involves controlling what happens in a business.

2. Importance of accounting. Accounting is of importance to business for a number of reasons.

(*a*) It is the firm's information system;
(*b*) Most business decisions are based upon financial information;
(*c*) It provides a means of evaluating past decisions and a basis upon which proposals for future developments can be made;
(*d*) It provides an estimate of the value of a business.

3. Basic principles. Every business transaction involves providing goods or services in return for payment. The basic system used to record these transactions is double-entry book-keeping, in which the giving and receiving of goods and services results in debits and credits being recorded. A debit is entered in an account for goods or services received and a credit is entered when goods or services are given.

4. Procedure. The main steps in entering transactions made by a business are as follows.

(*a*) All transactions, e.g. sales, payments and purchases, have an original document, such as an invoice, receipt, or credit note.

(*b*) Transactions are recorded in books of original entry, such as a Journal or Day Book.

(*c*) Cash items are entered in a Cash Book, while other items are entered in a Ledger. These are the two main books of account.

(*d*) A Trial Balance is made, usually at the end of a month or at the end of a trading period, to prove that mathematical double-entries are made.

(*e*) Final Accounts are prepared, usually once a year, consisting of a Trading Account, Profit and Loss Account, and Balance Sheet.

5. Final Accounts. The main indication of the financial health of a business is provided by its final accounts, normally prepared once a year.

(*a*) A Trading Account is prepared to establish the overall profit (Gross Profit) of the business. The Gross Profit is the difference between the turnover (i.e. total sales of the business) and the cost of those sales.

Trading Account for year ending 31 March, 19–

	£		£
Opening Stock	6,000	Sales	75,000
Purchases	50,000	Less sales returns	4,000
	56,000	Total turnover	71,000
Less closing stock	10,000		
Cost of materials sold	46,000		
Costs (rent, heat, etc)	6,000		
Gross Profit	19,000		
	71,000		71,000

The Gross Profit of £19,000 in the example above is found by deducting the total cost of sales (£46,000 plus operating costs such as rent, rates, heating, and lighting) from total turnover (£71,000).

(*b*) A Profit & Loss Account is a statement of the progress of the business over a 12 month period. It is prepared by taking the Gross Profit and then deducting all overheads (e.g. rent, rates, lighting). Any income earned from activities other than the business, such as commission or rent, is added, and this results in the business's Net Profit. The Companies Act, 1985, makes it compulsory for companies to produce a Profit & Loss Account.

Profit & Loss Account for year ending 31 March, 19–

	£		£
Rent and rates	3,000	Gross Profit	19,000
Salaries and wages	10,500	(from Trading Account)	
Lighting and heating	2,500	Commission received	1,500
Advertising	500		
Sundries	500		
Net Profit	3,500		
	20,500		20,500

The Gross Profit of £19,000 has commission of £1,500 added to it. The firm's various expenses, such as lighting, heating, and advertising, are deducted, leaving a net, or 'clean', profit of £3,500 which has been earned during the year.

An Appropriation Account has to be prepared by partnerships and limited companies as part of the Profit & Loss Account, to show the distribution of the net profit between the partners or shareholders.

(*c*) A Balance Sheet is a statement – not an account – which provides a summary of the final position of a business for shareholders, employees, and others. A Balance Sheet can be produced at any time, but is usually prepared at the end of the financial year to show a business's assets and liabilities at that time.

Balance Sheet as at 31 March, 19–

Liabilities	£		*Assets* Cost	£ Depreciation	*Book* Value
		Fixed assets:			
Capital	16,000	Fixtures & fittings	10,000	4,000	6,000
Net Profit	3,500	Vehicles	8,000	3,000	5,000
Long-term liability:			18,000	7,000	11,000
Bank Loan	6,000				
Current liabilities:		Current Assets:			
		Cash			5,300
Creditors	7,550	Stock			10,000
VAT	2,250	Debtors			9,000
	35,300				35,300

Index